BRITISH DANCE BANDS

(1920 - 1949)

ON

12-INCH LONG-PLAYING RECORDS

SUPPLEMENT TO ORIGINAL EDITION

Compiled By Edward Towler

PUBLISHED BY

GENERAL GRAMOPHONE PUBLICATIONS LIMITED

177-179 Kenton Road, Harrow, Middlesex, HA3 OHA

ISBN 0 902470 14 0

Printed in Great Britain

by

Frank Richards, Harrow, Middlesex

INTRODUCTION

Since the original edition of this Catalogue was published in 1985, there has been little abatement in the issue of long-playing albums by vintage British dance bands. They continue to appear with a frequency, and in a variety of compilations and packages, undreamt of a decade or so ago. Happily, it is a welcome state of affairs, that must reflect the continuing interest in the bands and their musicians, singers and arrangers, but at the same time, the influx of so many new albums has rendered the Catalogue deficient of much relevant information. To varying degrees, it might be said that most works of reference are invalidated by subsequent developments, but it is hoped that this Supplement will help to remedy the deficiency and provide the collector with a valid and up-to-date source of reference.

In layout and arrangement, the Supplement follows a similar format to that used in the Catalogue, and contains details of nearly 70 new albums which have appeared in the period since the Catalogue was completed. A few of these are of foreign origin, but it is believed they are still currently available as 'imports' in the United Kingdom through a number of retail outlets. In addition, there are details of several albums which were inadvertently omitted from the original Catalogue, and in the main these are grouped together under albums C142-C148. I am grateful to those collectors who have pointed out these omissions, and in particular I should like to thank Derek Beeby and Ken Deacon who kindly provided most of the details. Although the albums are no longer generally available, it is felt that their interest value not only justifies their inclusion, but that the Catalogue would be incomplete without them.

The identification of vocalists is a subject that continues to provoke interest and research, and this of course is both desirable and essential if the identities of singers who entered a recording studio over half a century and more ago are to be positively established. As a consequence of such activity some corrections are necessary to vocalists shown in the Catalogue, and some hitherto 'unknown' vocalists have been given an identity. Details of these are shown separately in these prefatory pages, together with some amendments to the Catalogue of a more general nature, and in this connection I should like to express my thanks to Colin Brown for pointing out Dorothy Carless's presence on the Geraldo recording of "Begin The Beguine"; and to Alasdair Fenton for correcting the singers shown for Jack Hylton and Ronnie Munro recordings.

The prectice adopted in the Catalogue of showing dated of birth and death under bandleader headings has been maintained in the Supplement. With the passage of time it has become increasingly difficult ot ascertain some of this information with accuracy. All too often in the past, the demise of a musician, singer or bandleader of the pre-war era has passed un-noticed by the National press. Fortunately, the press today is generally more sympathethic, and usually accords a deceased artist of the period the honour of an obituary, but is was not always so. I am therefore grateful to Doug Wilkins, who has carried out considerable and painstaking research in these matters, and who kindly offered to provide from his files any information that was lacking. As a consequence, Doug has filled in a number of gaps, and provided much additional information to that shown in the Catalogue, some of which may possibly be appearing in print for the first time. I am much indebted to him for his assistance.

The Supplement also contains an Index of Vocalists, which covers both the Catalogue and the Supplement, and which will be found in Section 4. It is perhaps a restricted one, and shows details of the bands which a singer is featured, together with the album numbers in which recordings are contained. Whilst a more comprehensive index, showning individual tune titles might be desirable, it will be appreciated - since a singer is to be heard on a majority of titles - that an index on such lines would probably result in a volume as copious in content as the Catalogue and Supplement together! It is hoped, however, that the Index will facilitate reference for the reader interested in the work of a particular singer.

Finally, in addition to those already mentioned, I should like to acknowledge the assistance I have received in the preparation of the Supplement from Colin Brown (Decca), Les Ovenden and Geoff Williams (Victor Silvester Appreciation Society), who all provided information of one kind or another, and whose help and co-operation has been much appreciated.

Higham, Kent.
June 1987

Edward Towler

NOTE - DELETIONS

Albums which are now deleted are marked with an asterisk (*) immediately after the record company's catalogue number. Many of them however may still be found in shops that specialise in second-hand records. Alternatively, it is often possible to acquire records that are no longer generally available by advertising in the classified columns of GRAMOPHONE, 177-179 Kenton Road, Harrow, Middlesex HA3 OHA.

ABBREVIATIONS

The following abbreviations have been used in the Supplement:

78rmp Record Labels

Bcst	Broadcast	Oriole	Oriole
Br	Brunswick	Pan	Panachord
Col	Columbia	Par	Parlophone
Dec	Decca	Reg	Regal
EBW	Edison Bell Winner	Rex	Rex
HMV	His Master's Voice	RZ	Regal Zonophone
Imp	Imperial	Ster	Stermo
Met	Metropole	Zon	Zonophone
Oct	Octacros		

Musical Instruments

alto sax	alto saxophone	pno	piano
bass sax	bass saxophone	tbn	trombone
clar	clarinet	tenor sax	tenor saxophone
drs	drums	tpt	trumpet
gtr	guitar	vln	violin

General

Acc/Accomp	Accompaniment/ Accompained (by)	LANS/LANS HSE	Lansdowne/Lansdowne House
Acc Bd	Accordeon Band	LPAB	London Piano Accordeon Band
Aldw Plyrs	Aldwych Players		
b	born	Med	Medley
BBCDO	BBC Dance Orchestra	NMDO	New Mayfair Dance Orchestra
Bcstrs	Broadcasters		
Bd	Band	N/V	Non-Vocal
c	circa	ODB&M	Organ, Dance Band & Me
comp	composer(s)	O/Or/Orch	Orchestra
D.O.	Dance Orchestra	Pt	Part
Dir	Directed (by)	Rest	Restaurant
Frds	Friends	RRCS	Radio Rhythm Club Sextet
GBS	Gaumont-British Symphony	Sel/Seln	Selection
GTO	Gaucho Tango Orchestra	Ser	Serenaders
Hse	House	Sext	Sextet
Inst/Instr	Instrumental	SHO	Savoy Hotel Orpheans
		Sw Qrt	Swing Quartet

REISSUES

The following albums, which are included in the original edition of the Catalogue, have been reissued under the titles and release numbers shown. The albums' contents are unchanged.

Album 109 THE YOUNG MANTOVANI 1935-39 : World Records SH 386
Reissued as: The Golden Age Of THE YOUNG MANTOVANI 1935-39 on EMI GX 41 2545 1

Album 116 FELIX MENDELSSOHN'S HAWAIIAN SERENADERS - Evergreens-Hawaiian Style : World Records SH 394
Reissued as: The Golden Age Of FELIX MENDELSSOHN'S HAWAIIAN SERENADERS On EMI GX 41 2544 1

Album 145 JACK PAYNE AND HIS BBC DANCE ORCHESTRA : World Records SH 143
Reissued as: The Golden Age Of JACK PAYNE WITH HIS BBC DANCE ORCHESTRA on EMI GX 41 2535 1

Album C24 HAPPY DAYS ARE HERE AGAIN - Hits Of The Thirties : World Records SH 337
Reissued under same title on EMI Retrospect Series EG 26 0628 1

Album C66 BRITAIN CAN TAKE IT : World Records SH 213
Reissued as: KEEP SMILING THROUGH on EMI GX 41 2532 1

Album C111 SOPHIE TUCKER - Some Of These Days : World Records SH 234
Reissued as: The Golden Age Of SOPHIE TUCKER on EMI GX 41 2533 1

ADDITIONS AND AMENDMENTS TO THE ORIGINAL EDITION

The following amendments should be made in respect of the titles indicated in the albums shown, which are included in the original edition of the Catalogue.

Page 4 Album 7 AMBROSE/"I Don't Know Why (I Just Do)" - The singer accompanying Sam Browne is Phyllis Robins (not Ella Logan)

Page 11 Album C140 AMBROSE/"This Is The Army, Mister Jones" - Amend recording date to 8 Dec 1943

Page 19 Album 25 BILLY COTTON AND HIS BAND - Crazy Weather

Details of this album were included in the Catalogue in advance of the album's release, and it is regretted that some of the information provided has proved to be inaccurate. The vocalists on the following titles should read as shown hereunder. The singers on the remaining titles are as shown in the Catalogue.

Crazy Weather (Chips Chippendall)
Two Cigarettes In The Dark (Chips Chippendall)
Judy (Chips Chippendall)
I Was In The Mood (Sam Browne)
The Man From Harlem (Ellis Jackson & Teddy Foster)
Who Made Little Boy Blue? (Alan Breeze)

Page 42 Album C10 GERALDO/"Begin The Beguine" - The singer is Dorothy Carless (not Eve Becke)

Page 57 Album C127 HENRY HALL/"Jack O' Diamonds" - Amend vocal details to read: Trio incl. Dan Donovan

Page 60 Album C75 HARRY HUDSON/"Happy Feet" - Add vocalists: Al Bowlly & Les Allen The month of recording is September (1930)

Page 71 Album C12 JACK HYLTON/"I'm Like A Sailor" - The singer is Sam Browne (not Pat O'Malley)

Page 72 Album 95 JACK JACKSON/"Come On, Be Happy" - Add Jack Jackson to vocal details, i.e.: Al Bowlly & Jack Jackson

Page 85 Album C135 PERCIVAL MACKEY/"Thanks For The Buggy Ride" - The"Unknown" singer is Fred Douglas

Page 87 Album C140 MANTOVANI/"It's A Million To One" - Add vocalist: Alan Kane

Page 91 Album C8 RONNIE MUNRO/"Cinderalla (Stay In My Arms)" - The singer is Hughie Diamond (not Jack Cooper)

Page 105 Album C19 RAY NOBLE/"Nasty Man" - Dorothy Carless's presence on this 1934 recording would seem to be doubtful. It is believed that Miss Carless made her first recording in 1938

Page 109 Album 149 JACK PAYNE AND HIS BAND 1939-1940
All reference to this album should be deleted. Due to a change in their marketing arrangements, Decca are now issuing their Recollections series of albums on the London label, and this record, which was originally scheduled for release as Decca RFL 50, will not now be issued.

Page 114 Album C140 OSCAR RABIN/"They Call Me A Dreamer" - Add full date of recording: 10 Jul 1940

Page 129 Album 169 GEORGE SHEARING/"A Pretty Girl Is Like A Melody" and "More Than You Know" - These titles which are shown as "Unissued" on 78rpm records were in fact issued on Decca F8181

Page 144 Album C33 LEON VAN STRATEN/"The Lady's In Love With You"- The "Unknown" singer is Julie Dawn

Page 146 Album C131 RHYTHM RASCALS/"Nobody's Sweetheart"- Add vocalist: Sam Browne

Page 189 Album C140 The London Shows - The War Years (2-Record Set)
This album was originally scheduled for release in Decca's Recollections series as RFLD 47, but due to the previously mentioned change in Decca's marketing arrangements, the album was subsequently issued on the London label with a release number of RECDL 1. The album's contents are unchanged.

Collections C28 to C33 (Those Dance Bands Years) - These albums were also issued singly on World Records SH 361 - SH 366 (now deleted)

Collections C35 to C41 (The Great British Dance Bands Play The Hits Of World War II) - These albums were also issued singly on World Records SH 343-SH 349 (now deleted)

SECTION 1

Explanatory Notes

This part of the Supplement follows a similar format to that adopted in the original edition of the Catalogue, and contains details of 78rpm recordings by vintage British dance bands which have been reissued of 12-inch long-playing records since the original Catalogue was compiled in May 1985. Details are shown under individual bandleaders' names and in accordance with the following column headings, which are referred to after the first page of the Section by the numbers shown is parenthesis at the top of each column:-

(1) LP Album Ref No	(2) Tune Title (and Vocalist)	(3) Date of Recording	(4) 78rpm Label and Catalogue No	(5) Cross Reference to Titles duplicated in other Albums

Column (1) shows the LP Album Reference Number applying to this Supplement (it is not the record company's catalogue number). To maintain continuity, the numbering used in the Supplement continues in sequence from the numbers last used in the Catalogue. Thus, albums in which all the tracks are by one particular band, and which have been designated "Complete Albums", have been given a sequence of numbers commencing at 194. Albums of "Collections", which contain tracks by different bands, and in some cases artists outside the scope of the Supplement, have been given a sequence of numbers commencing at C142. This arrangement avoids confusing albums in the supplement with those in the Catalogue, and so enables reference to be made in Column (5) to recordings that are also contained in the original Catalogue. Where such references are made, the album reference numbers are shown in parenthesis, e.g. (7) or (C102), thus indicating at a glance that the album referred to is included in the Catalogue and not in the Supplement (see example below).

Column (2) shows the Tune Title with the name of the vocalist in parenthesis. In instances where a vocalist has not been positively identified an entry of "Unknown" is shown. Titles that are entirely instrumental have been designated "Non-Vocal", which is abbreviated in the text to "N/V".

Column (3) shows the date the 78rpm recording was made; and Column (4) the 78rpm record label and catalogue number under which it was originally issued.

Details of Complete Albums are listed in album playing order. The full title is shown for each album, together with the record label and catalogue number.

Albums of Collections, which for identification have been given a reference number prefixed with the letter 'C', are summarised in Section 2 of the Supplement. Details of recordings included in these Collections by any one particular band are, however, shown in full in Section 1 under the bandleader's name. In instances where a recording contained in a Collection has also been included in a Complete Album by that band, the Collection reference number is shown in Column (5) of Section 1 against the relevant title in the Complete Album. For example, for Ambrose recording of "Dancing In The Dark" which is contained in Collection C180 is shown in Section 1 under album 195, in which it is also included, as follows (but since the recording was also included in album 7 in the Catalogue, reference to that album is also shown in Column (5) in parenthesis, as referred to in paragraph 2 above):

(1)	(2)	(3)	(4)	(5)
195	The Golden Age Of AMBROSE AND HIS ORCHESTRA : EMI GX 41 2525 1			
	Dancing In The Dark (Sam Browne)	11 Jan 1932	HMV B6132	(7) C180

Conversely, the reference number of the Complete Album (i.e. 195) is shown against the tune title in Collection C180 in Section 2. Details of other recordings by the band which are contained in Collections, but which are not included in a Complete Album, are shown in Section 1 after the Complete Album listings. These recordings are listed in consecutive order of the Collection reference numbers which are shown in Column (1), with any duplication of the title in another Collection shown in Column (5). For example, the Ambrose recording of "Coming In On A Wing And A Prayer" which is contained in Collections C146 and C169, but which is not included in a Complete Album by the band, is shown in Section 1 as follows:

(1)	(2)	(3)	(4)	(5)
	Titles contained in Collections only:			
	AMBROSE AND HIS ORCHESTRA:			
C146	Coming In On A Wing And A Prayer (Anne Shelton)	1 Jul 1943	Dec F8328	C169

In cases where a band has not been accorded an album to itself, details of its recordings, which must necessarily all be contained in Collections, are listed under the bandleader's name in the form illustrated above.

The reader interested in a particular title shown in Section 1 as being contained in a Collection, and who wishes to ascertain details of other titles in the album, can do so by referring to the corresponding Collection reference number in Section 2 of the Supplement.

E.T.

(1) LP Album Ref No	(2) Tune Title (and Vocalist)	(3) Date of Recording	(4) 78rpm Label & Cat. No	(5) Cross Reference to Titles duplicated in other Albums

AMBROSE
(b 15 September 1896; d 12 June 1971)

194 AMBROSE AND HIS ORCHESTRA 1928 To 1930 - 'S Wonderful : Saville SVL 181

'S Wonderful (N/V)	13 Nov 1928	Br 199	
Roll Away, Clouds (N/V)	13 Nov 1928	Br 199	
Louise (Eddie Grossbart)	9 Jul 1929	Dec M 49	
An Old Italian Love Song (Eddie Grossbart)	9 Jul 1929	Dec M 55	
I'll See You Again (Eddie Grossbart)	26 Jul 1929	Dec M 63	
If Love Were All (Eddie Grossbart)	26 Jul 1929	Dec M 63	
Singing In The Rain (N/V)	12 Sep 1929	Dec M 70	
Too Wonderful For Words (Lou Abelardo)	28 Oct 1929	Dec M 91	
Ain't Misbehavin' (Lou Abelardo)	28 Oct 1929	Dec M 93	
Am I Blue? (Lou Abelardo)	28 Oct 1929	Dec M 93	
Love Is A Dreamer (Lou Abelardo)	4 Nov 1929	Dec M102	
The Thought Never Entered My Head (Lou Abelardo)	12 Nov 1929	Dec M101	
She's Such A Comfort To Me (Lou Abelardo)	15 Nov 1929	Dec M101	
How Am I To Know? (Lou Abelardo)	30 Dec 1929	Dec M113	
My Sweeter Than Sweet (Lou Abelardo)	30 Dec 1929	Dec M112	
Piccolo Pete (Lou Abelardo)	2 Jan 1930	Dec M111	
Just You, Just Me (Lou Abelardo)	22 Jan 1930	Dec M115	
My Love Parade (Lou Abelardo)	29 Jan 1930	Dec M117	
A Little Kiss Each Morning (Sam Browne)	8 Feb 1930	Dec M120	
Lucky Me, Lovable You (Sam Browne)	13 Feb 1930	Dec M122	

Produced & Transferred by John Wadley — Sleeve Note by Brian Rust

195 The Golden Age Of AMBROSE AND HIS ORCHESTRA : EMI GX 41 2525 1

'Leven Thirty Saturday Night (Sam Browne)	22 May 1930	HMV B5847	(4 5 7 C75)
Cryin' For The Carolines (Sam Browne)	8 Apr 1930	HMV B5814	(5 7)
The Free And Easy (Sam Browne)	14 Jul 1930	HMV B5869	(5 7)
Stardust (N/V)	15 Jan 1931	HMV B5967	(7)
Blue Again (Sam Browne)	21 Feb 1931	HMV B5967	(7)
Bye Bye Blues (Sam Browne)	13 Oct 1930	HMV B5908	(7 C18)
Yes Yes (My Baby Said Yes) (Sam Browne & the Carlyle Cousins: Cecile Petrie, Pauline Lister and Lillian Taylor)	2 Oct 1931	HMV B6079	(7 C20 C21)
Whistling In The Dark (Sam Browne)	9 Jun 1931	HMV B6032	(7 C20)
I Don't Know Why (I Just Do) (Phyllis Robins & Sam Browne)	28 Nov 1931	HMV B6110	(7)
Dancing In The Dark (Sam Browne)	11 Jan 1932	HMV B6132	(7) C180
Soft Lights And Sweet Music (Sam Browne)	17 Jun 1932	HMV B6205	(7 C34)
When Yuba Plays The Rumba On The Tuba (Sam Browne)	1 Jun 1932	HMV B6190	(7)
Isn't It Romantic? (Sam Browne)	3 Nov 1932	HMV B6271	(7)
Pu-Leeze! Mister Hemingway (Elsie Carlisle)	22 Nov 1932	RZ MR 769	(7) C181

(1)	(2)	(3)	(4)	(5)
	Too Many Tears (Sam Browne)	2 Jun 1932	HMV B6181	(7)
	Let's Put Out The Lights And Go To Sleep (Anona Winn & Sam Browne)	26 Oct 1932	HMV B6261	(7 C139)
	Produced by Chris Ellis Remastered by John Wadley		Sleeve Note by Brian Rust	
196	AMBROSE AND HIS ORCHESTRA - I Only Have Eyes For You : Old Bean Records OLD 9			
	How Could We Be Wrong? (Sam Browne)	2 Nov 1933	Br 01622	
	Because It's Love (Sam Browne)	8 Mar 1934	Br 01729	
	Tick-Tock Town (N/V)	12 Jun 1934	Br 01790	(12)
	Stars Fell On Alabama (Sam Browne)	24 Oct 1934	Dec F5282	
	I Travel Alone (Sam Browne)	25 Oct 1934	Dec F5283	
	Lost In A Fog (Sam Browne)	25 Oct 1934	Dec F5282	
	I Only Have Eyes For You (Sam Browne)	8 Nov 1934	Dec F5302	
	Dames (Sam Browne)	8 Nov 1934	Dec F5302	(12)
	Winter Wonderland (Sam Browne)	14 Dec 1934	Dec F5370	
	If I Had A Million Dollars (Sam Browne)	14 Dec 1934	Dec F5363	
	If I Love Again (Sam Browne)	14 Dec 1934	Dec F5363	
	London On A Rainy Night (Sam Browne)	14 Dec 1934	Dec F5370	
	Maracas (N/V)	20 Mar 1935	Dec F5490	
	Copenhagen (N/V)	30 Jul 1935	Dec F5696	(12 C43)
	It's An Old Southern Custom (Jack Cooper)	9 Aug 1935	Dec F5648	(12)
	According To The Moonlight (Jack Cooper)	9 Aug 1935	Dec F5648	
	Top Hat, White Tie And Tails (Jack Cooper)	10 Oct 1935	Dec F5739	
	Isn't This A Lovely Day? (Jack Cooper)	10 Oct 1935	Dec F5739	(12)
	Produced & Transferred by John Wadley		Sleeve Note by Brian Rust	
	Titles contained in Collections only:			
	AMBROSE AND HIS ORCHESTRA:			
C146	Coming In On A Wing And A Prayer (Anne Shelton)	1 Jul 1943	Dec F8328	C169
C148	A Girl Friend Of A Boy Friend Of Mine (Sam Browne & Trio)	13 Oct 1930	HMV B5909	(C15)
C154	The Sun Has Got His Hat On (Sam Browne)	13 Jul 1932	HMV B6210	(C127)
C157	They Didn't Believe Me (Sam Browne & the Carlyle Cousins: Cecile Petrie, Pauline Lister and Lillian Taylor)	2 Oct 1931	HMV B6077	(7)
	She Didn't Say 'Yes' (Sam Browne)	23 Feb 1932	HMV B6153	
C159	No! No! A Thousand Times No (Elsie Carlisle & Sam Browne)	20 Nov 1934	Dec F5318	(C102)
	I'm Gonna Wash My Hands Of You (Elsie Carlisle & Sam Browne)	20 Nov 1934	Dec F5318	(C103)
	Home James, And Don't Spare The Horses (Elsie Carlisle)	11 Dec 1934	Dec F5371	(C102)
C160	Nevertheless (Sam Browne)	16 Sep 1931	HMV B6067	(5 6)
	My Romance (Sam Browne)	27 Oct 1932	Dec F6264	
	La Di Da Di Da (Sam Browne)	30 Nov 1933	Br 01656	
	The Very Thought Of You (Sam Browne)	11 May 1934	Br 01769	
	La Cucaracha (Sam Browne & Chorus)	24 Oct 1934	Dec F5283	
	Okay Toots (The Rhythm Sisters: Kay Munro-Smith, Jean Conibear and Helen Raymond)	14 Dec 1934	Dec F5364	

(1)	(2)	(3)	(4)	(5)
	Streamline Strut (N/V)	20 Mar 1935	Dec F5489	(10)
	B'Wanga (N/V)	15 Apr 1935	Dec F5529	(11)
	Life Begins When You're In Love (Jack Cooper)	20 Mar 1936	Dec F5933	(15)
	Hide And Seek (N/V)	29 Jun 1936	Dec F6023	
	Organ Grinder's Swing(Evelyn Dall)	14 Oct 1936	Dec F6141	
	Tarantula (N/V)	30 Dec 1936	Dec F6282	
	Swing Is In The Air (Evelyn Dall)	24 Mar 1937	Dec Unissued take (F6387)	
	Power House (N/V)	27 Jul 1937	Dec F6468	
	Voo Doo (N/V)	10 Feb 1939	Dec Unissued	
	Mr Reynard's Nightmare (N/V)	10 Feb 1939	Dec Unissued	(10)
	Tootin' Around (N/V)	10 Feb 1939	Dec Unissued	(10 C112)
	Beer Barrel Polka (Evelyn Dall)	7 Jun 1939	Dec F7077	(15)
	War Dance Of The Wooden Indians (N/V)	13 Jun 1939	Dec F7089	(11)
	The Penguin (N/V)	17 Jun 1939	Dec F7089	(10)
	If A Grey-Haired Lady Says 'How's Yer Father?'(Jack Cooper)	27 Nov 1939	Dec F7322	
C163	Happy Days Are Here Again (Lou Abelardo)	29 Jan 1930	Dec M117	(2)
	I'm In The Market For You (Sam Browne)	24 Apr 1930	HMV B5824	(3)
C169	My Wubba Dolly (Evelyn Dall) (Note: original issue as Evelyn Dall with Ambrose & His Orchestra)	6 Feb 1940	Dec F7410	
	The Shrine Of Saint Cecilia (Denny Dennis)	5 Mar 1942	Dec F8105	
	I Threw A Kiss In The Ocean (Dorothy Carless)	25 Jun 1942	Dec F8182	(14)
	The Cookhouse Serenade (Leslie Douglas)	7 Oct 1942	Dec F8213	
	Better Not Roll Those Blue Blue Eyes (Anne Shelton)	19 Jun 1943	Dec F8327	
	If I Had My Way (Jack Cooper)	26 Nov 1943	Dec F8389	
	An Hour Never Passes (George Melachrino)	31 Mar 1944	Dec F8421	
	More And More (Anne Shelton)	2 Mar 1945	Dec F8511	
C172	Breathless (Leslie Douglas)	15 Sep 1942	Dec F8193	
C174	Rehearsing A Lullaby (Elsie Carlisle)	30 May 1935	Dec F5572	
C176	Limehouse Blues (N/V)	8 Aug 1935	Dec F5696	(11 C81 C112)
C179	All Through The Night (Sam Browne)	23 May 1935	Dec F5539	

ARCADIANS DANCE ORCHESTRA

See under BERT FIRMAN

STANLEY BARNETT

197 MADAME TUSSAUD'S DANCE ORCHESTRA DIRECTED BY STANLEY BARNETT- Rockin' In Rhythm : Retrieval FG 408

	Rockin' In Rhythm (N/V)	22 Jun 1933	EBW A5572	(C49)
	Black-Eyed Susan Brown (Phyllis Robins)*	22 Jun 1933	EBW A5572	
	Jazz Cocktail (N/V)*	21 Jul 1933	EBW A5580	
	My Bluebird's Singing The Blues (Phyllis Robins)*	25 Jul 1933	EBW A5580	
	Mood Indigo (Phyllis Robins)	25 Jul 1933	EBW A5578	
	I Raised My Hat (Phyllis Robins)	25 Jul 1933	EBW A5578	
	Stevedore Stomp (N/V)*	8 Aug 1933	EBW A5590	
	Roll Up The Carpet (Nat Harris)*	8 Aug 1933	EBW A5590	

(1)	(2)	(3)	(4)	(5)
	Lighting (N/V)	19 Sep 1933	EBW A5597	
	You're Still In My Heart (Harry Bentley)	19 Sep 1933	EBW A5597	
	Wild Goose Chase (N/V)	12 Oct 1933	EBW A5609	
	Sophisticated Lady (Harry Bentley)	12 Oct 1933	EBW A5609	
	Echoes Of The Jungle (N/V)	17 Nov 1933	EBW A5617	
	Old Man Blues (Unknown)	17 Nov 1933	EBW A5617	
	We'll All Go Riding On A Rainbow (Dan Donovan & two others)	Jan 1934	EBW A5634	
	Old Fashioned Sweethearts (Dan Donovan)	Jan 1934	EBW A5634	
	Who Walks In When I Walk Out? (Annette Keith)	Feb 1934	EBW A5643	
	You're Gonna Lose Your Gal (Annette Keith)	Feb 1934	EBW A5643	

Produced by Ron Jewson & John R.T. Davies
Transferred & Remastered by John R.T. Davies   Sleeve Note by Sandy Forbes

Note: Titles marked with an asterisk (*) are shown in the album sleeve note as having been taken from test pressings. The commercially issued 78rpm release numbers have however been shown in the foregoing details, and there may therefore be some variation in the performances contained in the LP and those issued on 78rpm records.
It should also be noted that this album contains the entire recorded output of Madame Tussaud's Dance Orchestra.

THE BARNSTORMERS

C174	La Di Da Di Da (Leslie Sarony & Chorus)	Dec 1933	Ster 1344	

BBC DANCE ORCHESTRA

See under HENRY HALL and JACK PAYNE

HARRY BIDGOOD
(b late 1897; d 15 November 1957)

Harry Bidgood recorded under a number of different names, and directed various 'house' bands and recording groups during the 1930's and 40's. The following titles are amongst those made as leader of one of the popular accordeon bands of the period.

	PRIMO SCALA'S ACCORDEON BAND:			
C146	Roll Me Over (Unknown)	Aug 1944	Rex 10211	
	My Love Is Only For You (Kenny Noble)	18 Nov 1947	Dec F8828	
	PRIMO SCALA'S BANJO AND ACCORDEON BAND:			
C171	Jingle Bells (The Keynotes)	14 Jul 1948	Dec F8983	
C172	Underneath The Arches (The Keynotes)	14 Apr 1948	Dec F8954	(19)

STANLEY BLACK
(b 14 June 1913)

	STANLEY BLACK AND HIS MODERNISTS:			
C160	Swanee (N/V)	Sep 1931	Oriole P101	
	I Ain't Got Nobody (Nat Gonella)	Sep 1931	Oriole P101	

(1)	(2)	(3)	(4)	(5)

THE BLUE MOUNTAINEERS

C160	When We're Alone (Sam Browne)	17 May 1932	Bcst 3207	
	Sweet Sixteen And Never Been Kissed (Sam Browne & Nat Gonella)	10 Sep 1932	Bcst 3250	(C100)

PHILIP BUCHEL

PHILIP BUCHEL With SPIKE HUGHES AND HIS THREE BLIND MICE:
Philip Buchel (alto sax, tap dancing); Norman Payne (tpt); Eddie Carroll (pno); Alan Ferguson (gtr); Spike Hughes (bass)

C162	You Know What I'll Do (N/V)	5 Jul 1930	Dec F1856	
	Happy Feet (N/V)	5 Jul 1930	Dec F1856	

CASANI CLUB ORCHESTRA

See under CHARLIE KUNZ

GEORGE CHISHOLM
(b 29 March 1915)

	GEORGE CHISHOLM AND HIS JIVE FIVE:			
C142	Rosetta (N/V)	12 Oct 1938	Dec F7015	(C45 C72)
C143	You'll Always Be Mine (N/V)	12 Oct 1938	Dec F7015	(C72)
	GEORGE CHISHOLM AND HIS JIVE EIGHT:			
	Broadhurst Garden Blues (N/V)	25 May 1944	Dec F8458	

AL COLLINS
(b 1899; d 1964)

	AL COLLINS AND HIS ORCHESTRA:			
C174	Moon Over Miami (Barry Leary)	31 Jan 1936	Dec F5875	

BILLY COTTON
(b 6 May 1899; d 25 March 1969)

198 BILLY COTTON AND HIS BAND - Wakee Wakee! : Living Era AJA 5037

	Somebody Stole My Gal (Alan Breeze)	19 May 1933	RZ MR958	199
	Bugle Call Rag (N/V)	19 May 1933	RZ MR958	
	I'm Just Wild About Harry (Bruts Gonella & Chorus)	25 Nov 1932	RZ MR768	(22)
	Third Tiger Rag (Teddy Foster & Chorus)	11 Jul 1934	RZ MR1413	(25)
	Mood Indigo (N/V)	24 Jun 1933	RZ MR996	
	"That's A Good Girl" Selection (N/V) Fancy Our Meeting So Green Ooo-La-La	13 Oct 1933	RZ MR1125	
	It's Only A Paper Moon (Alan Breeze)	3 Jan 1934	RZ MR1190	
	Rhapsody In Blue, Parts 1 & 2 (N/V) (Solo piano by Arthur Sandford)	19 May 1933	RZ MR957	
	Skirts (Sam Browne)	18 Feb 1933	RZ MR866	
	"Falling For You" Selection Sweep (N/V) Mrs Bartholomew (N/V)	30 Jun 1933	RZ MR999	

(1)	(2)	(3)	(4)	(5)
	You Don't Understand (N/V)			
	Why Has A Cow Got Four Legs?			
	(Alan Breeze)			
	Best Wishes (Sam Browne)	7 Jul 1933	RZ MR996	
	St. Louis Blues (Teddy Foster)	14 Aug 1934	RZ MR1413	(24 25)
	She Was Only Somebody's Daughter (The Western Brothers & members of band)	17 Sep 1932	RZ MR658	(24)
	Night Owl (Alan Breeze)	3 Jan 1934	RZ MR1190	
	"Forty-Second Street" Film Selection	30 Jun 1933	RZ MR999	
	I'm Young And Healthy (N/V)			
	You're Getting To Be A Habit With Me (N/V)			
	Shuffle Off To Buffalo (N/V)			
	Forty-Second Street (N/V)			
	Smile, Darn Ya, Smile (Cyril Grantham & Trio)	4 Sep 1931	Col CB350	(22)

Produced by Kevin Daly & Tony Baldwin — Sleeve Note by Brian Rust

199 BILLY COTTON AND HIS BAND - Somebody Stole My Gal : Old Bean Records OLD 7

(1)	(2)	(3)	(4)	(5)
	I'm Young And Healthy (Alan Breeze)	11 Mar 1933	RZ MR875	
	Sweetheart (Alan Breeze)	18 Mar 1933	RZ MR891	
	One Little Word Led To Another (Sam Browne)	13 Jan 1933	RZ MR835	
	Doin' The Uptown Lowdown (Trio)	17 Dec 1933	RZ MR1189	
	Sophisticated Lady (N/V)	22 Aug 1933	RZ MR1035	
	Somebody Stole My Gal (Alan Breeze)	19 May 1933	RZ MR958	198
	Two Hearts On A Tree (Chips Chippendall)	30 Aug 1934	RZ MR1451	
	La Cucaracha (Alan Breeze)	21 Sep 1934	RZ MR1451	
	I've Had My Moments (Chips Chippendall)	14 Aug 1934	RZ MR1414	
	I'll Never Say "Never Again" Again (Chips Chippendall)	17 Aug 1935	RZ MR1812	(24)
	The Moon Was Yellow (Alan Breeze)	19 Jan 1935	RZ MR1585	
	What Harlem Is To Me (Alan Breeze)	15 Jul 1935	RZ MR1840	
	A Street In Old Seville (Chips Chippendall)	26 Mar 1935	RZ MR1669	
	Rhythm Mad (N/V)	26 Mar 1935	RZ MR1668	
	I'm On A See-Saw (Alan Browne)	8 Jan 1935	RZ MR1565	
	Dinah (Teddy Foster & Trio incl. (Chips Chippendall)	18 Sep 1935	RZ MR1946	
	Ev'ry Single Little Tingle Of My Heart (Chips Chippendall)	17 Aug 1935	RZ MR1812	
	Some Of These Days (Chips Chippendall)	18 Sep 1935	RZ MR1946	

Produced & Transferred by John Wadley — Sleeve Note by Tony Clarke

Titles contained in Collections only:

BILLY COTTON AND HIS BAND:

(1)	(2)	(3)	(4)	(5)
C146	I'm Going To Get Lit-Up (Alan Breeze)	6 May 1943	Rex 10180	
	Sailor, Who Are You Dreaming Of Tonight? (Alan Breeze)	27 Oct 1943	Rex 10193	
	I've Got A Lovely Bunch Of Coconuts (Alan Breeze)	9 May 1949	Dec F9149	
C161	Shoe Shine Boy (Jack Doyle?)	27 Aug 1936	RZ MR2189	
C163	It's The Girl (Cyril Grantham)	10 Oct 1931	Col CB374	(21)
	Too Many Tears (Sam Browne)	3 Jun 1932	Reg MR605	(22)

(1)	(2)	(3)	(4)	(5)
C167	I've Got Sixpence (Alan Breeze)	22 Apr 1941	Rex 9972	(C105)
	Ma, I Miss Your Apple Pie (Alan Breeze)	Jan 1942	Rex 10096	
	This Is The Army, Mr Jones (Alan Breeze)	27 Oct 1943	Rex 10191	

JOHNNY DENIS

JOHNNY DENIS AND HIS NOVELTY SWINGTET:

C172	Dream (Johnny Denis)	21 Sep 1945	Dec F8566	

LOUIS DE VRIES

(b 1906; d September 1935)

LOUIS DE VRIES AND HIS RHYTHM BOYS:

Louis De Vries (tpt); Lew Davis (tbn); Billy Amstell (clar); Monia Liter (pno); Don Stutely (bass)

C160	St. Louis Blues (N/V)	Jun 1935	Dec F5566	
	Moonglow (Brian Lawrence)	Jun 1935	Dec F5566	

JIMMY DORSEY

(b 29 February 1904; d 12 June 1957)

JIMMY DORSEY Accompanied By SPIKE HUGHES AND HIS THREE BLIND MICE:

Jimmy Dorsey (alto sax & clar); Claude Ivy (pno); Alan Ferguson (gtr); Spike Hughes (bass); Bill Harty (drs)

C162	I'm Just Wild About Harry (N/V)	15 Jul 1930	Dec F1876	(C46)
	After You've Gone (N/V)	15 Jul 1930	Dec F1876	(C46)
	Tiger Rag (MB1620-1) (N/V)	15 Jul 1930	Dec F1878	(C46)
	Tiger Rag (MB1620-2) (N/V)	15 Jul 1930	Dec F6142	
	St. Louis Blues (N/V)	15 Jul 1930	Dec F1878	(C46)

FRED ELIZALDE

(b 12 December 1907; d 16 January 1979)

	FRED ELIZALDE AND HIS MUSIC:			
C142	Clarinet Marmalade (N/V)	Aug 1927	Br 120	(29 30 C45 C75)
C143	Stomp Your Feet (N/V)	Aug 1927	Br 120	(29 30 C75)
	FRED ELIZALDE'S RHYTHMICIANS:			
C163	After The Sun Kissed The World Goodbye (Al Bowlly)	4 Dec 1929	Met 1241	(C89)

THE EMBASSY RHYTHM EIGHT

Max Goldberg (tpt); Lew Davis (tbn); Danny Polo (alto sax & clar); Billy Amstell (tenor sax); Bert Barnes (pno); Joe Brannelly (gtr); Dick Ball (bass); Max Bacon (drs)

C160	Hitchy Koo (N/V)	1 Feb 1935	Dec F5435	(C72)
	He's A Rag Picker (N/V)	1 Feb 1935	Dec F5435	(C72)

MIFF FERRIE

MIFF FERRIE AND HIS FERRYMEN:

C174	Sweetheart Of All My Dreams (N/V)	14 Jun 1945	Dec unissued take (F8569)	

(1)	(2)	(3)	(4)	(5)

BERT FIRMAN
(b 3 February 1906)

As Musical Director for the Zonophone label in the latter part of the 1920's, Bert Firman directed many of the various house bands whose recordings formed a large part of the Company's Popular catalogue. The following titles were recorded under his leadership.

	ARCADIANS DANCE ORCHESTRA:			
C148	Sunny Skies (N/V)	22 May 1928	Zon 5150	
	When I Met Connie In The Cornfield (Maurice Elwin)	5 Sep 1929	Zon 5459	(C55)
	THE RHYTHMIC EIGHT:			
C148	I Ain't Got Nobody (N/V)	23 Feb 1928	Zon 5097	(C53 C55)
	Can't Help Lovin' Dat Man (Maurice Elwin)	11 Jun 1928	Zon 5164	

ROY FOX
(b 25 October 1901; d 20 March 1982)

200 ROY FOX AND HIS BAND - Invitation To A Dance : Saville SVL 179

	Swaller Tail Coat (Sid Buckman & Chorus)	4 May 1934	Dec F[illegible]	
	True (Peggy Dell)	4 May 1934	Dec F3987	
	One Morning In May (Denny Dennis)	26 Mar 1934	Dec F3943	
	Drowsy Blues (N/V)	10 Jul 1934	Dec F5124	(37)
	Fair And Warmer (Sid Buckman)	11 Jul 1934	Dec F5114	
	You Oughta Be In Pictures (Denny Dennis)	26 Mar 1934	DEc F3943	(36)
	Jungle Drums (N/V)	10 Jul 1934	Dec F5124	(37)
	Soon (comp Fitzgerald, Lisbona) (Peggy Dell)	27 Sep 1934	Dec F5213	
	I'll String Along With You (Denny Dennis)	11 Jul 1934	Dec F5114	
	I Saw Stars (Sid Buckman)	27 Sep 1934	Dec F5212	
	What A Difference A Day Made (Denny Dennis)	28 Dec 1934	Dec F5391	
	I'm In Love (comp Simon, Mysels) (Peggy Dell)	15 Nov 1934	Dec F5314	
	Out In The Cold Again (Denny Dennis)	28 Sep 1934	Dec F5213	
	Dream Man (Make Me Dream Some More) (Peggy Dell)	4 Jan 1935	Dec F5373	
	I've Got An Invitation To A Dance (Denny Dennis)	4 Jan 1935	Dec F5373	
	If The Moon Turns Green (Sid Buckman)	15 Apr 1935	Dec F5519	
	San Felipe (Denny Dennis)	27 Jan 1935	Dec F5591	
	Accent On Youth (Denny Dennis)	21 Oct 1935	Dec F5767	
	Did You Ever Have A Feeling You're Flying? (Peggy Dell)	23 Aug 1935	Dec F5679	
	The Echo Of A Song (comp Konig, Mann, Edgar) (Denny Dennis)	12 Nov 1935	Dec F5795	

Produced & Transferred by John Wadley   Sleeve Note by Austin Clegg

201 The Golden Age OF ROY FOX AND HIS ORCHESTRA (1936-38) : EMI GX 41 2528 1

	Love Is A Dancing Thing (Denny Dennis)	4 Jan 1936	HMV BD5011	(40 41)
	Play, Orchestra, Play (Denny Dennis)	24 Jan 1936	HMV BD5025	(41)

(1)	(2)	(3)	(4)	(5)
	Let's Face The Music And Dance (Denny Dennis)	6 Apr 1936	HMV BD5053	(41) C180
	South Sea Island Magic (Denny Dennis)	12 Sep 1936	HMV BD5108	(41)
	Whispering, Part 1 (Denny Dennis & the Whisperers: Mary Lee & Barry Gray)	16 Nov 1936	HMV BD 391	(40 41 C34)
	Whispering, Part 2 (Mary Lee & the Cubs: Les Lambert, Ivor Mairants & Harry Gold)	16 Nov 1936	HMV BD 391	(40 41 C34)
	The Night Is Young And You're So Beautiful (Barry Gray)	20 Feb 1937	HMV BD5185	(41)
	Love And Learn (Mary Lee)	22 Mar 1937	HMV BD5194	(41)
	(I've Got) Beginner's Luck (Mary Lee)	29 May 1937	HMV BD5224	(41)
	I've Got My Love To Keep Me Warm (Denny Dennis)	21 Jun 1937	HMV BD5233	(41)
	Fifty Million Robins Can't Be Wrong (Mary Lee)	2 Jul 1937	HMV BD5239	(41)
	Can I Forget You? (Barry Gray)	1 Oct 1937	HMV BD5270	(41 C9 C141)
	Things Are Looking Up (Denny Dennis)	15 Dec 1937	HMV BD5309	(41)
	Roses In December (Denny Dennis)	15 Dec 1937	HMV BD5309	(41)
	You Leave Me Breathless (Denny Dennis)	9 Aug 1938	HMV BD5396	(41)
	You Went To My Head (Mary Lee)	9 Aug 1938	HMV BD5397	(41)
	If It Rains, Who Cares? (Denny Dennis)	9 Aug 1938	HMV BD5396	(41)

Produced by Chris Ellis
Transferred & Remastered by John Wadley — Sleeve Note by Harry Francis

Titles contained in Collections only:

ROY FOX AND HIS BAND:

C160	A Peach Of A Pair (Al Bowlly)	28 Jan 1931	Dec F2233	
	I'm So Used To You Now (Al Bowlly)	1 Jun 1931	Dec F2352	
	Leave The Rest To Nature (Al Bowlly)	1 Jun 1931	Dec F2352	
C163	By The River Sainte Marie (Al Bowlly)	16 Jun 1931	Dec Unissued	(C90)
	The Wind's In The West (Peggy Dell, Jack Plant & the Cubs: Les Lambert, Ivor Mairants and Harry Gold)	31 Oct 1933	Dec F3727	(35)
C174	Ya Got Love (Al Bowlly)	21 Apr 1931	Dec F2329	(32)
	You're Telling Me (Sid Buckman & the Cubs: as above)	11 Nov 1932	Dec F3288	(33)

GERALDO

(b 10 August 1904; d 4 May 1974)

202 The Golden Age Of GERALDO ; EMI GX 41 2540 1

	GERALDO AND HIS ORCHESTRA:			
	On The Sentimental Side (Al Bowlly)	9 Sep 1938	HMV BD5402	
	I Hadn't Anyone Till You (Eve Becke)	9 Sep 1938	HMV BD5403	
	GERALDO AND THE SAVOY HOTEL ORCHESTRA:			
	You Gorgeous Dancing Doll (Cyril Grantham & Ensemble)	10 May 1940	Par F1733	
	Our Love Affair (Dorothy Carless)	12 Dec 1940	Par F1799	
	If I Only Had Wings (Sid Colin)	16 Nov 1940	Par F1791	
	I've Got My Eyes On You (Pat Taylor)	30 May 1940	Par F1741	
	Sweet Sue, Just You (Ensemble)	13 Jul 1940	Par F1761	
	There Goes That Song Again (Dorothy Carless)	25 Jun 1941	Par F1848	C181
	I Was Watching A Man Paint A Fence (George Evans)	29 Jun 1940	Par F1752	

(1)	(2)	(3)	(4)	(5)
	GERALDO AND HIS ORCHESTRA:			
	While The Music Plays On (Dorothy Carless)	8 Nov 1941	Par F1872	
	GERALDO AND THE SAVOY HOTEL ORCHESTRA:			
	Falling Leaves (Len Camber)	26 May 1941	Par F1841	
	GERALDO AND HIS ORCHESTRA:			
	Taking A Chance On Love (Doreen Villiers)	3 Jul 1943	Par F1986	
	Ragtime Cowboy Joe (Dorothy Carless, Johnny Green & Ensemble	4 Oct 1943	Par F1998	(50)
	Canzonetta (N/V) (Sole clarinet: Nat Temple)	2 Sep 1942	Par F1944	
	The Things We Did Last Summer (Carole Carr)	14 Jan 1947	Par F2205	
	Again (Eve Boswell)	29 Jun 1949	Par F2376	

Compiled by Hugh Palmer
Transferred by Peter Bown — Sleeve Note by Hugh Palmer

203 GERALDO AND HIS ORCHESTRA - Memories Of Gerry : Old Bean Records OLD 4

(1)	(2)	(3)	(4)	(5)
	Victory Walk (N/V)		-	
	Ragtime Cowboy Joe (Dorothy Carless & Cyril Shane)		-	
	Swinging With The Wind (George Evans)		-	
	Soft Shoe Shuffle (N/V)		-	
	My Ideal (Len Camber)		-	
	Tenement Symphony (Sally Douglas)		-	(53)
	I Wish I Could Fish (Jackie Hunter)		-	
	Heat Wave (N/V)		-	(53)
	Carry Me Back To Old Virginny (Archie Lewis)		-	
	Shoo Shoo Baby (Doreen Villiers & the Tophatters)		-	
	Concerto For Drums (N/V)		-	
	A Gal In Calico (Denny Vaughan)		-	
	Queer Street (N/V)		-	
	South American Way (Dorothy Carless)		-	(C99)
	Life Of The Party (Jackie Hunter)		-	
	Only Make Believe (Sally Douglas)		-	
	Little Jack Frost Get Lost (The Geraldtones)		-	(53)
	Oh, My Darling (Eve Boswell)		-	(53)

Produced & Transferred by Colin Brown — Sleeve Note by Freddy Clayton

Note: The tracks in this album were transcribed from privately owned Acetates of broadcast transcriptions made between 1944 and 1949.

204 GERALDO - Tip Top Tunes : Conifer CHD 135

(1)	(2)	(3)	(4)	(5)
	GERALDO AND HIS CONCERT ORCHESTRA/DANCE ORCHESTRA*			
	"Tip Top Tunes" Signature Tune (Announcement by David Miller)		-	
	My Heart Stood Still (N/V)		-	
	There's A Small Hotel (Carole Carr & Dick James)		-	
	Heather On The Heath (Joy Hoodless & Neville Williams)		-	

(1)	(2)	(3)	(4)	(5)
	*Rockin' Through Dixie (N/V)		-	
	Nature Boy (Archie Lewis)		-	
	What Is This Thing Called Love? (N/V)		-	
	I'm On A See-Saw (Carole Carr & Dick James)		-	
	<u>GERALDO STRINGS</u> (Following title only):			
	So Many Times Have I Cried Over You (Derrick Francis)		-	(53)
	*When Johnny Comes Marching Home (N/V)		-	
	Begin The Beguine (N/V)		-	
	<u>GERALDO STRINGS</u> (Following title only):			
	The Isle Of Innisfree (Bob Dale)		-	
	*Arkansas Traveller (N/V)		-	
	<u>GERALDO STRINGS</u>:			
	In A Little Spanish Town (N/V)		-	
	<u>GERALDO AND HIS CONCERT ORCHESTRA/DANCE ORCHESTRA*</u>:			
	The Nearness Of You (Carole Carr)		-	(53)
	*Top Hat, White Tie And Tails (N/V)		-	
	Autumn Concerto (Roy Edwards) (Solo piano by Geraldo)		-	
	*Hallelujah (N/V)		-	
	*Getting Nowhere (Carole Carr)		-	(53)

<u>Produced</u> by John Webb
<u>Transferred</u> by Colin Brown

<u>Sleeve Note</u> by Tony Clarke

Note: The tracks in this album were transcribed from privately owned acetates of broadcast transcriptions made between circa 1947 and 1954. As exact dates are not known, the album's contents, which must perforce contain some 1950's items, have therefore been shown in their entirety.

Titles contained in Collections only:

(1)	(2)	(3)	(4)	(5)
	<u>GERALDO AND HIS ORCHESTRA</u>:			
C156	Begin The Beguine (Dorothy Carless)	3 May 1939	HMV BD5482	(C10)
	<u>GERALDO AND THE SAVOY HOTEL ORCHESTRA</u>:			
	Ridin' High (Len Camber & Ensemble)	12 Dec 1940	Par F1801	(C10)
	<u>GERALDO AND HIS ORCHESTRA</u>:			
	Don't Fence Me In (Johnny Green & Three Boys and A Girl)	6 Apr 1945	Par F2068	(C10)
	<u>GERALDO AND HIS GAUCHO TANGO ORCHESTRA</u>:			
C165	Yira, Yira (Monte Rey - sung in Spanish)		-	
	Vida Mia (Monte Rey - sung in Spanish)		-	
	Donde (Monte Rey)		-	
	<u>GERALDO AND HIS ORCHESTRA</u>:			
	Without A Song (Monte Rey & the Ovaltineys)		-	
	Beyond The Blue Horizon (Monte Rey & the Ovaltineys)*		-	
	I Surrender Dear (Monte Rey & the Radio Three: Kay Cavendish, Joy Worth and Ann Carring)		-	
	In My Little Red Book (Monte Rey & the Radio Three: as above)		-	
	Balloons (Monte Rey & the Ovaltineys)*		-	
	(Note: The tracks in album C165 were transcribed from privately owned acetates of recordings made for commercial radio stations between 1937 and 1939. Titles marked * also feature Sidney Torch at the organ.)			
C167	I Couldn't Sleep A Wink Last Night (Johnny Green)	10 May 1944	Par F2025	

(1)	(2)	(3)	(4)	(5)
C174	Will You Remember (Sweetheart)? (Cyril Grantham)	5 Jun 1937	Dec F6411	
	GERALDO AND THE SAVOY HOTEL ORCHESTRA:			
C181	You've Done Something To My Heart (Gwen Jones)	2 Dec 1939	Col FB2344	(C127)

CARROLL GIBBONS
(b 4 January 1903; d 10 May 1954)

205 CARROLL GIBBONS AND THE SAVOY HOTEL ORPHEANS - Brighter Than The Sun : Saville SVL 174

All My Life (Jack Plant)	7 Jan 1932	Col CB403	
You're The Kind Of A Baby For Me (Al Bowlly)	21 Jan 1932	Col CB403	
Kiss By Kiss (Al Bowlly & the Carlyle Cousins: Cecile Petrie, Pauline Lister & Lillian Taylor)*	18 Feb 1932	Col CB429	(C117)
Sailing On The Robert E. Lee (Al Bowlly)*	24 Mar 1932	Col CB443	(C117)
One Hour With You (Jack Plant)	20 Apr 1932	Col CB448	
What Makes You So Adorable? (Al Bowlly)	11 May 1932	Col CB469	
By Special Permission Of The Copyright Owners (I Love You) (Les Allen)	14 Jun 1932	Col CB469	
After Tonight We Say Goodbye (Les Allen)	5 Oct 1932	Col CB511	
I Wish I Knew A Bigger Word Than Love (Maurice Elwin)	18 Jan 1933	Col CB564	
What More Can I Ask? (Maurice Elwin)	18 Jan 1933	Col CB559	
Brighter Than The Sun (Maurice Elwin)	18 Jan 1933	Col CB559	
It's Gonna Be You (Maurice Elwin)	20 Feb 1933	Col CB587	
Oceans Of Time (Harry Bentley)	21 Dec 1933	Col CB709	
You're Gonna Lose Your Gal (Harry Bentley)	16 Jan 1934	Col CB709	
One Morning In May (Harry Bentley)	7 Apr 1934	Col CB742	
May I? (Harry Bentley)	25 May 1934	Col CB760	
The Beat O' My Heart (Esther Coleman)	25 May 1934	Col CB760	
So Help Me (Harry Bentley)	6 Jul 1934	Col CB773	
I Saw Stars (Harry Bentley)	23 Oct 1934	Col CB803	
For All We Know (Harry Bentley)	23 Oct 1934	Col CB803	C163

* Original issues as The Masqueraders

Produced & Transferred by John Wadley — Sleeve Note by Harry Bridges

206 The Golden Age Of CARROLL GIBBONS : EMI GX 41 2526 1

CARROLL GIBBONS AND HIS BOY FRIENDS:			
On The Air (Cecile Petrie)	7 Nov 1932	Col DB1001	(56)
SAVOY HOTEL ORPHEANS:			
Dancing In The Dark (Jack Plant)	16 Jan 1932	Col CB407	(55 56 C12)
CARROLL GIBBONS AND HIS BOY FRIENDS:			
Home (N/V)	24 Feb 1932	Col DB789	(56)
Tony's Wife (N/V)	28 Jun 1933	Col DB1163	(56)
With Thee I Swing (N/V)	3 Feb 1937	Col FB1644	(56)
I Double Dare You (N/V)	26 Jan 1938	Col FB1893	(56)
CARROLL GIBBONS AND THE SAVOY HOTEL ORPHEANS:			
Sixty Seconds Got Together (George Melachrino)	6 Oct 1938	Col FB2059	C180

(1)	(2)	(3)	(4)	(5)
	I Have Eyes (Anne Lenner)	6 Feb 1939	Col FB2161	
	Wishing (George Melachrino)	8 Jun 1939	Col FB2244	
	A Nightingale Sang In Berkeley Square (Anne Lenner)	24 Jun 1940	Col FB2466	(56 C130)
	I'm Nobody's Baby (Anne Lenner)	8 Oct 1940	Col FB2511	(56)
	Room Five-Hundred-And-Four (Anne Lenner)	12 Feb 1941	Col FB2579	(56 C37)
	Come Happy Day (Unknown)	11 Jun 1941	Col FB2641	
	CARROLL GIBBONS (Piano Solos):			
	Let's Be Sensible (Carroll Gibbons)	28 Aug 1941	Col FB2700	(56)
	When Day Is Done (N/V)	21 Jul 1942	Col FB2839	(56)
	CARROLL GIBBONS AND THE SAVOY HOTEL ORPHEANS:			
	I'm Going To Get Lit-Up (Carroll Gibbons)	19 Apr 1943	Col FB2923	(56)

Produced by Chris Ellis   Sleeve Note by Hubert Gregg

207 CARROLL GIBBONS - Carroll Re-Calls The Tunes : EMI Retrospect Series SH 509

CARROLL GIBBONS (Piano & Vocal*):			
Carroll Re-Calls The tunes No.1, Pt.1 The Lady Is A Tramp Sweet Sue, Just You California, Here I Come	19 Apr 1943	Col FB2922	
Carroll Re-Calls The Tunes No.1, Pt.2 Babette I Can't Give You Anything But Love Dinah	19 Apr 1943	Col FB2922	
Carroll Re-Calls The Tunes No.2, Pt.1 Ain't Misbehavin' Stormy Weather Exactly Like You	Jun 1943	Col FB2948	
Carroll Re-Calls The Tunes No.2, Pt.2 Oh Me, Oh My They Didn't Believe Me Cheek To Cheek	Jun 1943	Col FB2948	
Carroll Re-Calls The Tunes No.3, Pt.1 In The Still Of The Night Two Sleepy People Rosalie	Jan 1944	Col FB3016	
Solitude	c Feb 1942	Col FB2785	
Time On My Hands	4 Mar 1941	Col FB2785	
Manhattan Holiday	16 Nov 1937	Col FB1836	
Bubbling Over	Apr 1937	Col FB1677	
I Cried For You (*Carroll Gibbons)	5 Mar 1940	Col FB2403	
Carroll Re-Calls The Tunes No.3, Pt.2 Somebody Loves Me These Foolish Things I'll See You In My Dreams	Jan 1944	Col FB3016	
Reminiscing In Waltz Time, Part 1 Diane I'll See You Again Kiss Me Again	Oct 1941	Col FB2718	
Reminiscing In Waltz Time, Part 2 Alice Blue Gown Speak To Me Of Love Marcheta	Oct 1941	Col FB2718	
Tribute To Fats Waller, Part 1 Ain't Misbehavin' Honeysuckle Rose	15 May 1944	Col FB3074	

(1)	(2)	(3)	(4)	(5)
	Tribute To Fats Waller, Part 2	15 May 1944	Col FB3074	
	I've Got A Feeling I'm Falling			
	Keepin' Out Of Mischief Now			
	Summer Rain	16 Nov 1937	Col FB1836	
	Smoke Gets In Your Eyes	11 May 1942	Col FB2804	
	The Way You Look Tonight	11 May 1942	Col FB2804	
	Moonbeams Dance	Apr 1937	Col FB1677	
	I Want The Waiter (*Carroll Gibbons)	5 Mar 1940	Col FB2403	

Produced & Transferred by Chris Ellis   Sleeve Note by Brian Rust

Titles contained in Collections only:

(1)	(2)	(3)	(4)	(5)
	NEW MAYFAIR DANCE ORCHESTRA (Directed by CARROLL GIBBONS):			
C163	Good Little, Bad Little You (Eddie Collis)	19 Feb 1929	HMV B5597	(C121)
	SAVOY HOTEL ORPHEANS:			
C153	Sweet And Lovely (Al Bowlly)	29 Oct 1931	Col CB376	(54 C51 C85 C93)
	CARROLL GIBBONS AND THE SAVOY HOTEL ORPHEANS:			
C155	Rosalie (George Melachrino)	24 Jan 1938	Col FB1884	
C156	It's D'Lovely (Anne Lenner & George Melachrino)	7 Sep 1938	Col FB2032	(C10)
	I've Got My Eyes On You (Anne Lenner)	25 May 1940	Col FB2451	(C10)
	Do I Love You, Do I? (Anne Lenner)	24 Apr 1941	Col FB2625	(C10)
	You'd Be So Nice To Come Home To (Edna Kaye)	12 May 1943	Col FB2935	(C10)
	SAVOY HOTEL ORPHEANS:			
C163	My Silent Love (Les Allen)	19 Sep 1932	Col CB504	(55)
	CARROLL GIBBONS AND THE SAVOY HOTEL ORPHEANS Accompanying Larry Adler (Harmonica):			
C166	Rhapsody In Blue, Part 1	28 May 1935	RZ MR1820	
	Rhapsody In Blue, Part 2	6 Jul 1935	RZ MR1820	
	CARROLL GIBBONS AND THE SAVOY HOTEL ORPHEANS:			
C167	Mary Lou (Denny Vaughan)	8 May 1946	Col FB3220	
C181	The Moon Got In My Eyes (Anne Lenner)	4 Nov 1937	Col FB1829	(19)

NAT GONELLA
(b 7 March 1908)

208 NAT GONELLA AND HIS GEORGIANS - Naturally Gonella : Conifer CHD 129

(1)	(2)	(3)	(4)	(5)
	Yeah Man (Nat Gonella & Chorus)	25 Nov 1935	Par F347	
	Truckin' (Nat Gonella)	6 Oct 1935	Par F283	210
	Hot Lips (Ensemble)	15 Jul 1935	Par F193	
	The Sheik Of Araby (Jimmy Messini & Nat Gonella)	29 Oct 1935	Par F317	
	Black Coffee (Nat Gonella)	24 Jul 1935	Par F210	
	Blow, Gabriel, Blow (Nat Gonella & Chorus)	15 Jul 1935	Par F193	(C10)
	Capri Caprice (Isle Of Capri) (Nat Gonella)	30 Oct 1935	Par F317	
	Oh! Peter (You're So Nice) (Nat Gonella & Chorus)	6 Oct 1935	Par F284	
	Georgia Rockin' Chair (Nat Gonella)	20 Oct 1935	Par F346	
	Lazy River (Nat Gonella)	24 Jul 1935	Par F210	(C49)
	Sweet And Hot (Nat Gonella & Chorus)	11 Sep 1935	Par F227	(60)
	Pidgin' English Hula (Nat Gonella)	6 Oct 1935	Par F284	
	Squareface (Nat Gonella)	11 Sep 1935	Par F227	(60)
	Jealous (Jimmy Messini)	30 Oct 1935	Par F319	
	Japanese Sandman (N/V)	25 Nov 1935	Par F347	210

(1)	(2)	(3)	(4)	(5)
	The Ghost Of Dinah (Nat Gonella & Chorus)	6 Oct 1935	Par F283	
	Jig Time (Nat Gonella)	7 Jun 1935	Par F180	
	Gonna Wed That Gal O' Mine (Nat Gonella)	3 May 1935	Par F162	
	The Peanut Vendor (Nat Gonella)	7 Jun 1935	Par F180	
	Sophisticated Lady (Jimmy Messini)	29 Oct 1935	Par F319	

Produced, Remastered & Transferred by Colin Brown — Sleeve Note by Frank Stapleton

209 NAT GONELLA AND HIS GEORGIANS - How'm I Doin? : Old Bean Records OLD 11

	Ol' Man Mose (Nat Gonella & Chorus)	2 Apr 1936	Par F442	(61)
	How'm I Doin'? (Nat Gonella)	6 Jul 1936	Par F524	
	Mama Don't Allow It (Nat Gonella & Chorus)	27 Feb 1936	Par F414	
	Blue Turning Grey Over You (Nat Gonella)	10 Jan 1936	Par F369	210
	Lazy Rhythm (N/V)	6 Jul 1936	Par F524	
	Fan It (Nat Gonella)	27 Feb 1936	Par F415	
	You Rascal, (Nat Gonella)	29 Jan 1936	Par F393	
	Get Hot (N/V)	28 May 1936	Par F486	
	Kicking The Gong Around (Nat Gonella)	20 May 1936	Par F463	
	Bye Bye Blues (Nat Gonella)	10 Dec 1936	Par F639	(61)
	The Music Goes Round And Around (Nat Gonella)	21 Jan 1936	Par F386	
	I'm Confessin' (That I Love You) (Nat Gonella)	8 Oct 1936	Par F569	210
	Someone Stole Gabriel's Horn (Nat Gonella)	10 Jan 1936	Par F370	(61)
	Lady Be Good (N/V)	8 Oct 1936	Par F639	
	His Old Cornet (Nat Gonella)	20 May 1936	Par F463	
	How Long, How Long Blues (Nat Gonella)	27 Feb 1936	Par F415	
	I Want To Be Happy (N/V)	10 Jan 1936	Par F369	(60)
	Sweet Music Man (Nat Gonella)	21 Jan 1936	Par F386	
	Old Man River (Nat Gonella)	10 Jan 1936	Par F370	
	Swinging To Those Lies (It's A Sin To Tell A Lie) (Nat Gonella)	2 Dec 1936	Par F623	

Produced & Transferred by Colin Brown — Sleeve Note by Freddy Clayton

210 The Golden Age OF NAT GONELLA AND HIS GEORGIANS : EMI GX 41 2536 1

	Nagasaki (Nat Gonella & Band)	3 May 1935	Par F161	(C14)
	I'm Confessin' (That I Love You) (Nat Gonella)	8 Oct 1936	Par F569	209
	Japanese Sandman (N/V)	25 Nov 1935	Par F347	208
	Fascinating Rhythm (Nat Gonella)	3 Jul 1935	Par F192	
	Blue Turning Grey Over You (Nat Gonella)	10 Jan 1936	Par F369	209
	Hesitation Blues (Nat Gonella)	3 Jul 1935	Par F192	
	The Toy Trumpet (N/V)	2 Sep 1937	Par F880	
	The Skeleton In The Cupboard (Nat Gonella)	7 Jan 1937	Par F645	
	Ain't Misbehavin'(Nat Gonella)	8 Oct 1936	Par F593	
	Singing The Blues (N/V)	29 Jan 1936	Par F392	
	I Can't Dance (I Got Ants In My Pants) (Nat Gonella & Band)	15 Sep 1937	Par F909	
	Truckin' (Nat Gonella)	6 Oct 1935	Par F283	208

(1)	(2)	(3)	(4)	(5)
	Caravan (N/V)	15 Sep 1937	Par F904	
	NAT GONELLA AND HIS NEW GEORGIANS:			
	I'm Nobody's Baby (Nat Gonella)	4 Oct 1940	Col FB2523	
	Can't Get Indiana Off My Mind (Nat Gonella)	4 Oct 1940	Col FB2523	
	NAT GONELLA (tpt) With Norman Stenfalt (pno) & Johnny Marks (drs):			
	The Sheik Of Araby (Nat Gonella)	9 Apr 1941	Col FB2620	

Compiled by Hugh Palmer
Transferred by John R.T. Davies

Sleeve Note by Hugh Palmer

Titles contained in Collections only:

(1)	(2)	(3)	(4)	(5)
	NAT GONELLA With Instrumental Accomp:			
C142	Georgia On My Mind (Nat Gonella)	15 May 1934	Dec F3992	(59 C45 C80 C115)
	NAT GONELLA AND HIS GEORGIANS:			
C167	One Meat Ball (Helen Mack & Nat Gonella)	22 Jul 1946	Dec F8663	(C104) C174
C172	Murder (Nat Gonella)	22 Jul 1946	Dec F8691	(C100 C125)
C174	Gnat Jump (N/V)	20 Jul 1945	Dec Unissued take (F8599)	(C100 C125)

STEPHANE GRAPPELLY
(b 26 January 1908)

(1)	(2)	(3)	(4)	(5)
	STEPHANE GRAPPELLY AND HIS MUSICIANS:			
C151	Noel Brings The Swing (N/V)	28 Feb 1941	Dec F7841	C173
	I Never Knew (comp Pitts, Egan, Marsh) (N/V)	28 Feb 1941	Dec F8128	
	Sweet Sue, Just You (N/V)	28 Feb 1941	Dec F7841	C173
	STEPHANE GRAPPELLY AND HIS QUARTET:			
	Jive Bomber (N/V)	9 Apr 1941	Dec F7865	C173
	Dinah (N/V)	9 Apr 1941	Dec F7865	C173
	STAPHANE GRAPPELLY AND HIS QUINTET:			
	Au Revoir (N/V)	28 Jan 1943	Dec F8451	
	Stardust (N/V)	28 Jan 1943	Dec F8451	
	STEPHANE GRAPPELLY AND HIS MUSICIANS:			
C173	After You've Gone (N/V)	30 Jul 1940	Dec F7570	(C44)
	Stephane's Tune (N/V)	30 Jul 1940	Dec F7570	
	Tiger Rag (N/V)	28 Feb 1941	Dec F7787	
	Stephane's Blues (N/V)	28 Feb 1941	Dec F7787	
	STAPHANE GRAPPELLY AND HIS QUARTET:			
	Heavenly Music (Beryl Davis)	6 Oct 1943	Dec F8375	
	Star Eyes (Beryl Davis)	6 Oct 1943	Dec F8375	
	My Heart Tells Me (Dave Fullerton)	3 Dec 1943	Dec F8392	
	I Never Mention Your Name (Dave Fullerton)	3 Dec 1943	Dec F8392	
	I'm Confessin' (That I Love You) (Beryl Davis)	10 Jun 1944	Dec Unissued	
	Someday, Sweetheart (Beryl Davis)	10 Jun 1944	Dec F9745	
	Don't You Know I Care? (Beryl Davis)	29 Nov 1944	Dec F8492	
	STEPHANE GRAPPELLY AND HIS QUINTET:			
	Liza (All The Clouds'll Roll Away) (N/V)	20 Aug 1942	Dec F8204	
	The Folks Who Live On The Hill (Dave Fullerton)	20 Aug 1942	Dec F8204	
	When I Look At You (Beryl Davis)	7 Jul 1943	Dec F8334	
	Weep No More, My Lady (Beryl Davis)	7 Jul 1943	Dec F8333	
	Three O'Clock In The Morning (N/V)	7 Jul 1943	Dec F8334	
	That Old Black Magic (Beryl Davis)	7 Jul 1943	Dec F8333	

(1)	(2)	(3)	(4)	(5)

HENRY HALL
(b 2 May 1898)

(1)	(2)	(3)	(4)	(5)
211	HENRY HALL AND THE BBC DANCE ORCHESTRA - What A Perfect Combination : Saville SVL 178			
	What A Perfect Combination (Les Allen)	4 Feb 1933	Col CB568	
	In The Moonlight (Les Allen)	4 Feb 1933	Col CB568	
	My Darling (Sam Browne)	14 Feb 1933	Col CB573	
	Just So You'll Remember (Sam Browne)	14 Feb 1933	Col CB573	
	Twenty Million People (Les Allen)	14 Mar 1933	Col CB585	
	In A Little Second Hand Store (Les Allen)	8 Jul 1933	Col CB643	
	The Day You Came Along (Les Allen)	16 Oct 1933	Col CB672	
	Thanks (Les Allen)	16 Oct 1933	Col CB672	
	That's Another Scottish Story (Bud Flanagan & Chesney Allen)	13 Nov 1933	Col CB684	
	Roaming (Bud Flanagan & Chesney Allen)	13 Nov 1933	Col CB684	
	On A Steamer Coming Over (Phyllis Robins & Les Allen)	12 Dec 1933	Col CB699	
	I'll String Along With You (Les Allen)	3 Jul 1934	Col CB770	
	Little Valley In The Mountains (Les Allen)	3 Jul 1934	Col CB770	
	Love In Bloom (Les Allen)	18 Aug 1934	Col CB778	
	With My Eyes Wide Open I'm Dreaming (Les Allen)	18 Aug 1934	Col CB778	
	How's Chances (Dan Donovan)	12 Feb 1935	Col FB1024	(C3 C20)
	Samum (A Symphonic Fox-Trot) (N/V)	23 Feb 1935	Col FB1035	
	Sidewalks Of Cuba (N/V)	23 Feb 1935	Col FB1035	
	Say The Word And It's Yours (Dan Donovan)	23 Oct 1935	Col FB1195	
	Everything's In Rhythm With My Heart (Dan Donovan)	23 Oct 1935	Col FB1195	

Produced & Transferred by John Wadley — Sleeve Note by Tony Clarke

Titles contained in Collections only:

(1)	(2)	(3)	(4)	(5)
	BBC DANCE ORCHESTRA DIRECTED BY HENRY HALL:			
C154	Who's Afraid Of The Big Bad Wolf? (Les Allen & Trio)	16 Oct 1933	Col CB669	(C16)
C156	Anything Goes (Dan Donovan)	30 May 1935	Col FB1068	(C10)
	Easy To Love (Dan Donovan)	23 Jan 1937	Col FB1626	(C10)
	I've Got You Under My Skin (Dan Donovan)	23 Jan 1937	Col FB1626	(C10)
C157	The Song Is You (Les Allen)	4 Apr 1933	Col CB598	(C9 C141)
C163	How Can You Say "No"? (Les Allen)	4 Nov 1932	col CB532	(64)
	HENRY HALL AND HIS GLENEAGLES HOTEL BAND:			
C174	I Was True (Tommy Whitefoot)	10 Jan 1932	Dec F2774	
	BBC DANCE ORCHESTRA DIRECTED BY HENRY HALL:			
C176	The Teddy Bears' Picnic (Val Rosing)	28 Sep 1932	Col DB955	(67 C24 C34)
C180	The Music Goes 'Round And Around (George Elrick)	7 Jan 1936	Col FB1288	(66)

JACK HARRIS
(b 29 August 1901; d 10 January 1976)

(1)	(2)	(3)	(4)	(5)
	JACK HARRIS AND HIS ORCHESTRA:			
C160	You Brought A New Kind Of Love To Me (Harry Bentley?)	5 Jul 1930	Dec F1868	

(1)	(2)	(3)	(4)	(5)
	The Moon Is Low (Harry Bentley?)	16 Jul 1930	Dec F1871	
C174	On The Sunny Side Of The Street (Unknown)	26 May 1930	Dec Unissued	(C80)

HATCHETT'S SWINGTETTE

(1)	(2)	(3)	(4)	(5)
C172	Papa's In Bed With His Breeches On (Dorothy Carless)	7 Apr 1941	Dec F7860	
C173	You Made Me Love You (Beryl Davis)	29 Dec 1939	Dec Unissued take (F7904)	
	Alexander's Ragtime Band (Beryl Davis)	29 Dec 1939	Dec F7904	
	Ting-A-Ling (The Waltz Of The Bells) (Beryl Davis)	29 Dec 1939	Dec F7336	
	Scatterbrain (Beryl Davis)	29 Dec 1939	Dec F7336	(70)
	It's A Hap-Hap-Happy Day (Beryl Davis)	25 Jan 1940	Dec F7398	
	Bluebirds In The Moonlight (Beryl Davis)	25 Jan 1940	Dec F7398	
	Oh, Johnny, Oh Johnny, Oh! (Beryl Davis)	25 Jan 1940	Dec F7405	
	I Got Rhythm (N/V)	19 Mar 1940	Dec F7500	(70)
	Lady Be Good (N/V)	19 Mar 1940	Dec F7500	(70)
	In the Mood (Beryl Davis)	19 Mar 1940	Dec F7450	(70)
	Playmates (Beryl Davis)	19 Apr 1940	Dec F7470	
	Oh! By Jingo, Oh! By Gee (Beryl Davis)	19 Apr 1940	Dec F7470	(70)
	The Sheik Of Araby (N/V)	8 Jul 1940	Dec F7761	(70)
	I Said "No" (Billie Campbell)	8 Apr 1942	Dec F8140	
C174	Beat Me Daddy, Eight To A Bar (Dorothy Carless)	19 Nov 1940	Dec F7697	(70 C107) C175

TED HEATH
(b 30 March 1902; d 18 November 1969)

TED HEATH AND HIS MUSIC:

(1)	(2)	(3)	(4)	(5)
C168	Mountain Greenery (N/V)	Nov 1946	Dec F8756	
	Sabre Dance (N/V)	Mar 1948	Dec F8886	

PATRICK 'SPIKE' HUGHES
(b 19 October 1908; d 2 February 1987)

(1)	(2)	(3)	(4)	(5)
	SPIKE HUGHES AND HIS DANCE ORCHESTRA:			
C142	The Moochi (N/V)	2 Apr 1930	Dec F1787	(74)
	SPIKE HUGHES AND HIS ORCHESTRA:			
C143	Doan' You Grieve (N/V)	Dec 1932	Dec F3399	
	SPIKE HUGHES AND HIS DANCE ORCHESTRA:			
C162	Poor Butterfly (Val Rosing)	29 Apr 1930	Dec F1815	
	Kalua (N/V)	27 Jun 1930	Dec F1816	(C49)
	Dancing Time (N/V)	27 Jun 1930	Dec F1816	
	I Like To Do Things For You (N/V)	27 Jun 1930	Dec F1844	
	Happy Feet (N/V)	27 Jun 1930	Dec F1844	
	Harlem Madness(N/V)	16 Jul 1930	Dec F1861	
	Blue Turning Grey Over You (Val Rosing)	16 Jul 1930	Dec F1861	
	Margie (N/V)	16 Jul 1930	Dec F1815	
	Cinderella Brown (N/V)	16 Jul 1930	Dec F1880	

See also under PHILIP BUCHEL and JIMMY DORSEY

(1)	(2)	(3)	(4)	(5)

JACK HYLTON
(b 2 July 1892; d 29 January 1965)

212 JACK HYLTON AND HIS ORCHESTRA - I'm In A Dancing Mood: EMI Retrospect Series SH 505

(1)	(2)	(3)	(4)	(5)
	I'll Never Say "Never Again" Again (Brian Lawrence)	15 Jul 1935	HMV BD204	(93)
	She's A Latin From Manhattan (Pat O'Malley)	26 Aug 1935	HMV BD212	
	About A Quarter To Nine (Sam Browne)	26 Aug 1935	HMV BD212	
	Rose Room (N/V)	25 Aug 1936	HMV BD5128	(90)
	I'm In A Dancing Mood (Bert Yarlett)	5 Nov 1936	HMV BD5136	
	At The Balalaika (Bert Yarlett)	10 Jan 1937	HMV BD5165	
	Boo-Hoo (The Swingtette: Frances Jewel, Dorothy McCarthy, Ben Lake and Gene Lanham	6 Apr 1937	HMV BD5201	
	September In The Rain (Tom Wareing)	7 May 1937	HMV BD5216	(93)
	Love Live Forever And Rule My Heart (Bert Yarlett)	13 May 1937	HMV BD5217	
	Girls Were Made To Love And Kiss (Bert Yarlett)	13 May 1937	HMV Unissued	
	Nice People (Sid Buckman)	31 Jan 1939	HMV BD5455	
	You Must Have Been A Beautiful Baby (Bruce Trent)	31 Jan 1939	HMV BD5455	
	Jeepers Creepers (Primrose Orrock)	8 Mar 1939	HMV BD5465	(90)
	Beer Barrel Polka (Bruce Trent)	25 May 1939	HMV BD5490	
	My Prayer (Peggy Dell)	24 Jul 1939	HMV BD5508	(90 91)
	Day In, Day Out (Dolly Elsie)	6 Nov 1939	HMV BD5539	(90)
	So Deep Is The Night (Sam Browne)	22 Dec 1939	HMV BD5554	
	Roadhouse Revels/The Melody Maker (N/V)	23 Dec 1939	HMV BD5557	
	Rosita (Her Name Was Rosita) (Denny Dennis)	1 Feb 1940	HMV BD5562	
	Let The People Sing (Celia Lipton)	1 Feb 1940	HMV BD5562	

Produced, Complied & Transferred by Chris Ellis

Sleeve Note by Tony Clarke

Titles contained in Collections only:

JACK HYLTON AND HIS ORCHESTRA:

(1)	(2)	(3)	(4)	(5)
C143	Some Of These Days (Billy Munn)	16 Sep 1933	Dec F3767	(87 C112)
C144	Chinese Laundry Blues (George Formby)*	1 Jul 1932	Dec F3079	(C61 C62 C98) C154 C170
	The Old Kitchen Kettle (George Formby)	13 Oct 1932	Dec F3222	(C60) C170
	Why Don't Women Like Me? (George Formby)*	29 Jan 1933	Dec F3524	(C61) C170
	Running Round The Fountains In Trafalgar Square (George Formby)*	29 Jan 1933	Dec F3524	C170
	Sitting On The Ice At The Ice Rink (George Formby)*	29 Jan 1933	Dec F3458	(C60) C170
C145	Do De O Do (George Formby)*	1 Jul 1932	Dec F3079	(C60 C62 C98) C170
	I Told My Baby With My Ukulele (George Formby)*	13 Oct 1932	Dec F3219	(C61 C62) C170

(*These titles were originally issued under George Formby's name, without reference to Jack Hylton & His Orchestra. The accompaniment on "Chinese Laundry Blues" and "Do De O Do" is by a contingent from the Hylton orchestra.)

(1)	(2)	(3)	(4)	(5)
C152	Painting The Clouds With Sunshine (trio)	25 Oct 1929	HMV B5722	(82 85 C19 C21)
C154	Is Izzy Azzy Wozz? (Max & Harry Nesbitt)	30 May 1929	HMV B5666	
C156	Let's Do It (Trio of Jack Hylton, Billy Ternent & Chappie D'Amato)	26 Mar 1929	HMV B5622	(C10)
	What Is This Thing Called Love? (Sam Browne)	26 Mar 1929	HMV B5621	(C10)
	Love For Sale (N/V)	2 Jul 1931	HMV B6046	(C10)
	You're The Top (Eve Becke & Pat O'Malley)	6 Jun 1935	HMV BD172	(C10)
	My Heart Belongs To Daddy (Pat Kirkwood)	17 Nov 1939	HMV BD5538	(C10)
C158	Maybe It's Me (Jack Hylton)	19 Jul 1927	HMV B5314	
C163	Honeymoon Hotel (Trio of Pat O'Malley, Sonny Farrar and Billy Ternent)	27 Nov 1933	Dec F3806	(88 89)
C170	If You Don't Want The Goods, Don't Maul 'Em (George Formby)	13 Oct 1932	Dec F3219	(C60 C62)
	Levi's Monkey Mike (George Formby)	29 Jan 1933	Dec F3458	(C60)
	(The above two titles were originally issued under George Formby's name, without reference to Jack Hylton and his Orchestra)			
C179	They All Fall In Love (Trio of Pat O'Malley, Billy Ternent and Chappie D'Amato)	10 May 1930	HMV B5841	(C10)
C180	Don't Let That Moon Get Away (Bruce Trent)	13 Dec 1938	HMV BD5445	(92)

ROBERTO INGLEZ

(d 4 September 1977)

ROBERTO INGLEZ AND HIS ORCHESTRA:

C167	The Green Cockatoo (N/V)	c Jul 1946	Par F2183	(94)

JACK JACKSON

(b 20 February 1906; d 14 January 1978)

213 JACK JACKSON AND HIS ORCHESTRA at the Dorchester Hotel, London - Things Are Looking Up : Saville SVL 173

	Things Are Looking Up (Trio of Fred Latham and probably Jack Jackson & Chappie D'Amato)	6 Dec 1934	HMV B6564	
	Faint Harmony (Sam Costa)	16 Jan 1934	HMV B6448	
	Soon (Alberta Hunter)	12 Oct 1934	HMV B6520	(96)
	You Turned Your Head (Trio as previously)	1 Sep 1934	HMV B6522	(C6)
	Kiss Me Dear (Peggy Cochrane & Jack Jackson)	1 Sep 1934	HMV B6522	C163
	The Ache In My Heart (Peggy Cochrane)	1 Sep 1934	HMV B6521	
	Now That We're Sweethearts Again (Trio as previously)	12 Apr 1934	HMV B6479	
	Have A Little Dream On Me (Fred Latham)	22 Oct 1934	HMV B6537	
	Don't You Cry When We Say Goodbye (Trio as previously)	9 Nov 1934	HMV B6547	
	Lonely Feet (Trio as previously)	10 May 1934	HMV B6489	
	I'm On A See-Saw (Fred Latham)	12 Dec 1934	HMV B6565	
	Dancing With A Ghost (Trio as previously)	12 Dec 1934	HMV B6565	

(1)	(2)	(3)	(4)	(5)
	Play To Me Gypsy (Sam Costa)	16 Jan 1934	HMV B6448	C163
	A Lonely Singing Fool (Alberta Hunter)	22 Oct 1934	HMV B6536	(96)
	What's Good For The Goose (Jack Jackson)	8 Mar 1934	HMV B6473	
	Because It's Love (Fred Latham)	9 Apr 1934	HMV B6479	
	Old Faithful (Fred Latham & Band)	12 Oct 1934	HMV B6530	
	What Shall I Do? (Alberta Hunter)	22 Oct 1934	HMV B6536	(96)
	I Think I Can (Fred Latham)	6 Dec 1934	HMV B6564	
	Goodnight, Lovely Little Lady (Trio of Peggy Cochrane, Fred Latham and Jack Jackson)	10 May 1934	HMV B6489	

Produced & Transferred by John Wadley   Sleeve Note by Brian Rust

Titles contained in Collections only:

JACK JACKSON AND HIS ORCHESTRA:

C174	The New Swing Alphabet (Jack Jackson & Jack Cooper)	26 Nov 1937	Dec F6568	

JAZZ CLUB

See under MARK WHITE

KEN JOHNSON

(b 1911; d 8 March 1941)

KEN JOHNSON AND HIS WEST INDIAN DANCE ORCHESTRA:

C174	Snakehips Swing (N/V)	22 Sep 1938	Dec F6854	(C80 C81)

TEDDY JOYCE

(b 1904; d 10 February 1941)

TEDDY JOYCE AND HIS DANCE MUSIC:

C174	I Never Had A Chance (Jimmy Messini)	1 Jul 1934	Ster 1483	(C102)

FELIX KING

(b 27 March 1912; d 13 June 1982)

FELIX KING, HIS PIANO AND ORCHESTRA:

C174	What Do I Have to Do (To Make You Love Me?) (N/V)	19 Jun 1948	Dec F9035	

TOMMY KINSMAN

(b 1901; d 15 March 1984)

TOMMY KINSMAN AND HIS DANCE BAND:

C174	Stardust (N/V)	Jan 1937	Oct Unissued take (1360)	

THE KIT-CAT BAND

C178	There's A Rickety Rackety Shack (Eddie Collis)	5 Jan 1928	Col 4703	

(1)	(2)	(3)	(4)	(5)

CHARLIE KUNZ
(b 18 August 1896; d 17 March 1958)

214 CHARLIE KUNZ AND THE CASANI CLUB ORCHESTRA - Dance Your Way Through The Thirties : Joy Records D 286

	Unless (Harry Bentley)	Jan 1934	Ster 1354	
	There Was An Old Woman (Unknown)	Oct 1934	Ster 1529	
	Learn To Croon (Harry Bentley)	Aug 1933	Ster 1241	(98)
	Did My Heart Beat (Did I Fall In Love?) (Eve Becke)	Oct 1933	Ster 1271	
	Let's Sit This One Out (Eve Becke & Harry Bentley)	Jan 1934	Ster 1337	(98)
	Did You Ever See A Dream Walking? (Harry Bentley)	Jan 1934	Ster 1336	(98)
	She Fell For A Feller From "Oopasala" (George Buck & Chorus)	Jan 1935	Ster 1571	
	Dear Stranger (Harry Bentley)	Sep 1933	Ster 1262	
	When You're Over Sixty (And Feel Like Sweet Sixteen) (Unknown)	Nov 1933	Ster 1295	
	Moonstruck (Harry Bentley)	Aug 1933	Ster 1241	(98)
	By A Waterfull (Harry Bentley)	Dec 1933	Ster 1343	
	Roaming (Les Allen)	Nov 1933	Ster 1295	
	Doggone, I've Done It (Dawn Davis)	Feb 1934	Ster 1377	
	Lazybones (Phyllis Robins)	Aug 1933	Ster 1224	
	Memories Of Hours Spent With You (Harry Bentley)	Jun 1934	Ster 1455	
	I Raised My Hat (Phyllis Robins)	Aug 1933	Ster 1224	
	On The Good Ship Lollipop (The Carlyle Cousins: Cecile Petrie, Pauline Lister and Lillian Taylor)	Jun 1935	Rex 8521	(99)
	There's No Green Grass Round The Old North Pole (Harry Bentley & Chorus)	Dec 1934	Ster 1564	

Produced & Remastered by Colin Brown — Sleeve Note by John Gunn

Titles contained in Collections only:

	CHARLIE KUNZ (piano) With Rhythm Accompaniment:			
C172	Piano Medley No. D84 (1 Part) - A Garden In The Rain / Danger Ahead / I'll Make Up For Everything	21 Nov 1947	Dec F8827	
	CHARLIE KUNZ AND THE CASANI CLUB ORCHESTRA:			
C174	Crying My Heart Out For You (Vera Lynn)	Aug 1936	Rex 8860	(99)

SYDNEY KYTE
(b 1 June 1896; d 29 July 1981)

	SYDNEY KYTE AND HIS PICCADILLY HOTEL BAND:			
C174	Lazybones (Unknown)	18 Aug 1933	EBW Unissued take (5586)	

BRIAN LAWRENCE
(b 13 October 1908; d 11 September 1983)

	BRIAN LAWRENCE AND HIS LANSDOWNE ORCHESTRA:			
C174	You're Looking For Romance (I'm Looking For Love) (Brian Lawrence)	2 Sep 1937	Rex 9120	

(1)	(2)	(3)	(4)	(5)

LOUIS LEVY
(b 1893; d 18 August 1957)

215 LOUIS LEVY AND HIS CONCERT ORCHESTRA : Decca Ace Of Clubs ACL 1245*

(1)	(2)	(3)	(4)	(5)
	LOUIS LEVY AND HIS MUSIC FROM THE MOVIES:			
	Cole Porter Suite (Medley), Parts 1 to 4 (N/V)	c 2 Jan 1947	Dec K1633/ K1634	
	Night And Day/I Get A Kick Out Of You/ Begin The Beguine/My Heart Belongs To Daddy/In The Still Of The Night/Let's Do It/I've Got You Under My Skin/ Don't Fence Me In/Anything Goes			
	George Gershwin Suite (Medley), Parts 1 to 4 (N/V)	Nov 1948	Dec K2117/ K2118	
	Strike Up The Band/Embraceable You/ Do Do Do/Love Walked In/Swanee/ Someone to Watch Over Me/ 'S Wonderful/ I Got Rhythm/Bidin' My Time/But Not For Me/Somebody Loves Me/Of Thee I Sing			

Produced by Geoff Milne

Titles contained in Collections only:

(1)	(2)	(3)	(4)	(5)
	LOUIS LEVY AND HIS ORCHESTRA:			
C181	Says My Heart (Eve Becke)	Jul 1938	Col FB2023	(101 C20 C21)

PHILIP LEWIS
(b 1892; d December 1931)

(1)	(2)	(3)	(4)	(5)
	PHILIP LEWIS AND HIS ORCHESTRA:			
C148	Tiger Rag (N/V)	11 Sep 1929	Dec F1540	
	Button Up Your Overcoat (Maurice Elwin)	12 Oct 1929	Dec F1557	
	THE RHYTHM MANIACS DIRECTED BY PHILIP LEWIS:			
	That's A-Plenty (N/V)	25 Oct 1929	Dec F1573	(C49)

SYDNEY LIPTON
(b 4 January 1906)

(1)	(2)	(3)	(4)	(5)
	SYDNEY LIPTON AND HIS GROSVENOR HOUSE ORCHESTRA:			
C174	Supposin' (comp Evans, Butler, Damerell) (Chips Chippendall)	29 Aug 1936	Dec F6070	(104)

JOE LOSS
(b 22 June 1910)

216 JOE LOSS AND HIS BAND 1933-1934 - Isn't It Heavenly? : Conifer CHD 128

(1)	(2)	(3)	(4)	(5)
	Smoke Gets In Your Eyes (N/V)	c Nov 1934	Oct 1098	
	In Other Words We're Through (Jimmy Messini)	Mar 1934	EBW 5663	(C103)
	When The New Moon Shines (Trio)	c Nov 1934	Oct 1105	
	I Love You Truly (Jimmy Messini)	Apr 1934	EBW 5668	
	Let's Fall In Love (N/V)	Mar 1934	EBW 5663	(C80 C103)
	Ole Faithful (Harry Case) (*)	c Nov 1934	Oct 1098	
	There's A Ring Around The Moon (Jimmy Messini)	20 Nov 1933	EBW 5620	(C103)
	For You, Madonna (Chick Henderson)	22 Oct 1935	HMV BD294	

(1)	(2)	(3)	(4)	(5)
	Stars Fell On Alabama (N/V)	c Nov 1934	Oct 1105	(C102)
	Soon (N/V)	c Nov 1934	Oct 1099	
	Isn't It Heavenly? (Jimmy Messini)	19 Sep 1933	EBW 5594	(C102)
	Tina (N/V)	c Nov 1934	Oct 1099	
	One Morning In May (Jimmy Messini)	Apr 1934	EBW 5667	(C115)
	Don't Forget (N/V)	c Nov 1934	Oct 1104	
	Ending With A Kiss (Jimmy Messini)	Apr 1934	EBW 5667	
	The General's Fast Asleep (Chick Henderson & Trio)	22 Oct 1935	HMV BD294	(105 C8)
	The Continental (N/V)	c Nov 1934	Oct 1106	
	Under A Blanket Of Blue (Jimmy Messini)	19 Sep 1933	EBW 5594	

(*) This track is incorrectly shown on both the sleeve and record label as "La Cocaracha" (sic)

Produced, Remastered & Transferred by Colin Brown — Sleeve Note by Tony Clarke

217 The Golden Age Of JOE LOSS AND HIS ORCHESTRA : EMI GX 41 2529 1

(1)	(2)	(3)	(4)	(5)
	Over My Shoulder (Jimmy Messini)	31 Aug 1934	RZ MR1417	(105)
	Madam-Ah! La Marquise-Ah! (Clem Stevens & others)	4 Jun 1936	HMV BD5080	(105)
	The Scene Changes (Chick Henderson)	10 Jul 1936	HMV BD5084	(105 106)
	Let's Dance At The Make Believe Ballroom (The Blue Notes)	2 Feb 1937	RZ MR2351	(105 107)
	Sweet Sue, Just You (Chick Henderson)	2 Feb 1937	RZ MR2351	(105 106)
	Boo-Hoo (Betty Dale & The Blue Notes)	5 May 1937	RZ MR2449	(105)
	So Rare (Chick Henderson)	4 Sep 1937	RZ MR2527	(105 106)
	Please Be Kind (Chick Henderson)	8 Jun 1938	RZ MR2787	(105 106)
	I'm Gonna Lock My Heart And Throw Away The Key (Clem Stevens)	20 Aug 1938	RZ MR2816	(105 C24)
	Change Partners (Chick Henderson)	29 Oct 1938	RZ MR2920	(105 106) C180
	The Latin Quarter (N/V)	7 Jan 1939	RZ MR2966	(105)
	Little Sir Echo (Chick Henderson & Band)	8 May 1939	RZ MR3048	(105 106)
	Boomps-A-Daisy (Annette Mills & Chorus; Announcement by Joe Loss)	5 Jun 1939	RZ MR3072	(105)
	Are You Havin' Any Fun? (Chick Henderson, Clem Stevens & The Blue Notes)	28 Dec 1939	RZ MR3205	(105 106)
	At The Woodchoppers' Ball (N/V)	18 Jan 1940	RZ MR3243	(105 107)
	In The Mood (N/V)	18 Jan 1940	RZ MR3243	(105 107 C18)

Produced by Chris Ellis
Remastered by John Wadley — Sleeve Note by Brian Rust

218 JOE LOSS AND HIS ORCHESTRA - Remember Me? : EMI Retrospect Series SH 506

(1)	(2)	(3)	(4)	(5)
	There's A New World (Chick Henderson)	10 Sep 1936	HMV BD5110	
	A Nice Cup Of Tea (Chick Henderson)	27 Feb 1937	RZ MR2391	
	With Plenty Of Money And You (Chick Henderson)	1 Apr 1937	RZ MR2434	
	Hometown (Chick Henderson)	4 Sep 1937	RZ MR2528	
	Silent Film Memories, Part 2 - Ramona (N/V) Diane (N/V) Charmaine (N/V)	21 Sep 1937	RZ MR2635	

(1)	(2)	(3)	(4)	(5)
	Silent Film Memories, Part 1 - Felix Kept On Walking (N/V) The Sheik Of Araby (N/V) My Blue Heaven (N/V)	21 Sep 1937	RZ MR2635	
	Remember Me? (Chick Henderson)	20 Nov 1937	RZ MR2639	
	Early Talkie Memories, Part 2 - Lullaby Of Broadway (N/V) Tip-Toe Through The Tulips (N/V) If I Had A Talking Picture Of You (N/V)	9 Dec 1937	RZ MR2678	
	I Double Dare You (Chick Henderson)	5 Feb 1938	RZ MR2694	
	The Palais Glide, Part 1 - All By Yourself In The Moonlight (N/V) Horsey, Keep Your Tail Up (N/V) Poor Little Angeline (N/V)	12 Feb 1938	RZ MR2706	
	You're An Education (Chick Henderson)	9 Apr 1938	RZ MR2742	
	Cry, Baby, Cry (Sam Costa)*	10 May 1938	RZ MR2765	
	Penny Serenade (Monte Rey)	29 Oct 1938	RZ MR2906	
	You Go To My Head (Chick Henderson)	29 Oct 1938	RZ MR2906	
	The Chestnut Tree (Ensemble)	7 Jan 1939	RZ MR2966	
	And The Angels Sing (Chick Henderson)	9 Jun 1939	RZ MR3073	
	Boom! (Why Does My Heart Go Boom?) (Clem Stevens)	17 Jul 1939	EZ MR3114	
	Oh, You Crazy Moon (Chick Henderson)*	11 Oct 1939	RZ MR3159	
	Scatterbrain (Chick Henderson)	8 Dec 1939	RZ MR3199	
	Oh! Johnny, Oh! Johnny, Oh! (Shirley Lenner)	28 Dec 1939	RZ MR3205	

*Original issues as MEL ROSE AND HIS BAND

Produced, Compiled & Transferred by Chris Ellis   Sleeve Note by Brian Rust

219 JOE LOSS AND HIS ORCHESTRA - In The Mood With Joe : President Lucky Evergreen Series PLE 522

(1)	(2)	(3)	(4)	(5)
	In The Mood (N/V)	8 Aug 1941	HMV BD5705	
	Daddy (Bette Roberts)	21 Sep 1941	HMV BD5707	
	That Lovely Week-End (Chick Henderson)	10 Jan 1942	HMV BD5729	(C47)
	The Fur Trappers' Ball (N/V)	10 Sep 1942	HMV BD5777	
	You Made Me Care (Chick Henderson)	1 May 1940	HMV BD5588	
	Five O'Clock Whistle (Bette Roberts)	5 Feb 1941	HMV BD5663	
	Fan It (N/V)	28 Nov 1943	HMV BD5830	
	For All That I Care (Monte Rey)	5 Jun 1941	HMV BD5681	
	Yeah Man (Elizabeth Batey)	11 Mar 1943	HMV BD5794	
	Sweet Little Sweetheart (Chick Henderson)	21 Jun 1940	HMV BD5603	
	No, Mama, No! (Paula Green)	21 Jun 1940	HMV BD5603	
	Cornsilk (Chick Henderson)	21 Sep 1941	HMV BD5707	
	Six Lessons From Madame La Zonga (Paula Green)	9 Oct 1940	HMV BD5623	
	Memories Live Longer Than Dreams (Cyril Grantham)	8 Oct 1940	HMV BD5621	
	Cow Cow Boogie (Elizabeth Batey)	28 Jan 1944	HMV BD5836	
	If I Should Fall In Love Again (Chick Henderson)	1 May 1940	HMV BD5589	
	Amapola (Monte Rey)	5 Jun 1941	HMV BD5681	(107 C37)
	Let The Curtain Come Down (Chick Henderson)	1 May 1940	HMV BD5588	

Produced & Remastered by Colin Brown   Sleeve Note by Tony Clarke

(1)	(2)	(3)	(4)	(5)
	Titles contained in Collections only:			
	JOE LOSS AND HIS ORCHESTRA:			
C167	Let Him Go, Let Him Tarry (Elizabeth Batey?)	Jul 1945	HMV BD5901	
	JOE LOSS AND HIS BAND:			
C174	In A Little Rocky Valley (Jimmy Messini)	Mar 1934	EBW 5662	(C102)

BRAM MARTIN
(b 22 June 1901; d 18 July 1984)

(1)	(2)	(3)	(4)	(5)
	BRAM MARTIN AND HIS BAND:			
C174	The Waves Of The Ocean Are Whisp'ring Goodnight (Al Bowlly)	8 Jun 1939	Rex 9590	(C133)

BILLY MAYERL
(b 31 May 1902; d 26 March 1959)

(1)	(2)	(3)	(4)	(5)
	BILLY MAYERL (Piano Solo):			
C146	Room Five-Hundred-And-Four	21 Mar 1941	Dec F7812	

FELIX MENDELSSOHN
(b 23 September 1911; d 4 February 1952)

(1)	(2)	(3)	(4)	(5)
	FELIX MENDELSSOHN AND HIS HAWAIIAN SERENADERS:			
C167	Paradise Isle (Not Known)	c 26 Feb 1946	Col FB3198	

BILLY MERRIN
(b 22 February 1900; d 24 July 1980)

(1)	(2)	(3)	(4)	(5)
	BILLY MERRIN AND HIS COMMANDERS:			
C174	There's A Ring Around The Moon (Billy Merrin)	11 Mar 1932	Dec F2879	

RONNIE MUNRO
(b 1897)

(1)	(2)	(3)	(4)	(5)
	RONNIE MUNRO AND HIS ORCHESTRA Accompanying Larry Adler (Harmonica):			
C166	I've Got You Under My Skin	2 Jun 1937	Col FB1703	
	They All Laughed	2 Jun 1937	Col FB1714	
	I've Got My Love To Keep Me Warm/ Slumming On Park Avenue	12 Aug 1937	Col FB1753	
	Caravan	25 Sep 1937	Col FB1776	
	Night And Day/Tiger Rag	25 Sep 1937	Col FB1776	
	RONNIE MUNRO AND HIS ORCHESTRA:			
C180	Me And My Girl (Jack Cooper)	1 Jan 1938	HMV BD5324	(C127)

NEW MAYFAIR DANCE ORCHESTRA

See under CARROLL GIBBONS and RAY NOBLE

(1)	(2)	(3)	(4)	(5)

THE NIGHT CLUB KINGS

See under RAY NOBLE

RAY NOBLE
(b 17 December 1903; d 2 April 1978)

220	Al Bowlly - Goodnight Sweetheart : EMI Retrospect Series SH 502			
	NEW MAYFAIR DANCE ORCHESTRA:			
	I'm Telling The World She's Mine (Al Bowlly)	20 Nov 1930	HMV B5940	(118 136)
	Goodnight Sweetheart (Al Bowlly)	19 Feb 1931	HMV B5984	(118 133 139 140 C84) C153 C177
	Lazy Day (Al Bowlly)	11 Jun 1931	HMV B6031	(119 132 138 140 C17)
	Hang Out The Stars In Indiana (Al Bowlly)	25 Aug 1931	HMV B6058	(120 133 C85)
	RAY NOBLE AND HIS NEW MAYFAIR DANCE ORCHESTRA:			
	There's A Ring Around The Moon (Al Bowlly)	3 Mar 1932	HMV B6154	(121 136)
	Goodnight Vienna (Al Bowlly)	7 Apr 1932	HMV B6172	(121 136)
	I'll Do My Best To Make You Happy (Al Bowlly)	8 Sep 1932	HMV B6245	(122 132 135 139)
	Love Is The Sweetest Thing (Al Bowlly)	8 Sep 1932	HMV B6245	(122 133 139 C23 C84) C153
	RAY NOBLE AND HIS ORCHESTRA:			
	Wanderer (Al Bowlly)	12 Jan 1933	HMV B6306	(123 131 135 143 C85 C93)
	Maybe It's Because I Love You Too Much (Al Bowlly)	3 May 1933	HMV B6347	(125 132 135 C17)
	Shadow Waltz (Al Bowlly)	5 Jul 1933	HMV B6376	(125)
	I've Got To Sing A Torch Song (Al Bowlly)	5 Jul 1933	HMV B6375	(126 C85)
	Close Your Eyes (comp B. Petkere) (Al Bowlly)	7 Dec 1933	HMV B6441	(127 131 137 C17 C93)
	Unless (Al Bowlly)	1 Feb 1934	HMV B6453	(128 134)
	Who Walks In When I Walk Out? (take-2) (Al Bowlly)	1 Feb 1934	HMV B6453	(128 136)
	The Very Thought Of You (Al Bowlly)	21 Apr 1934	HMV B6482	(129 131 135 139) C153 C176
	I'll String Along With You (Al Bowlly)	28 Jun 1934	HMV B6503	(129 131 C14 C84 C93)
	Grinzing (Al Bowlly)	24 Aug 1934	HMV B6519	(130 138)
	Dreaming A Dream (Al Bowlly)	30 Aug 1934	HMV B6520	(130 132 135 C19)
	Sing As We Go (Al Bowlly)	30 Aug 1934	HMV B6514	(130)

Produced & Transferred by Chris Ellis   Sleeve Note by Ray Pallett

221	RAY NOBLE AND HIS ORCHESTRA Featuring Al Bowlly - Over On The Sunny Side : Old Bean Records OLD 6			
	That's What Life Is Made Of (Al Bowlly)	10 May 1933	HMV B6361	(125 134 139 C51)
	You're Mine, You (Al Bowlly)	16 Jun 1933	HMV B6370	(125 133)
	I Only Want One Girl (Al Bowlly)	20 Jun 1933	HMV B6366	(125 134)
	There's A Cabin In The Pines (Al Bowlly)	13 Jul 1933	HMV B6379	(126)
	My Hat's On The Side Of My Head (Al Bowlly)	27 Oct 1933	HMV B6421	(127 136)

(1)	(2)	(3)	(4)	(5)
	This Is Romance (Al Bowlly)	9 Nov 1933	HMV B6422	(127 133)
	Song Without Words (Al Bowlly)	29 Nov 1933	HMV B6438	(127)
	Have A Heart (Al Bowlly)	1 Feb 1934	HMV B6459	(128)
	Who Walks In When I Walk Out? (take-1) (Al Bowlly)	1 Feb 1934	HMV Unissued	(128 C70)
	Midnight And The Stars And You (Al Bowlly)	16 Feb 1934	HMV B6461	(128 133)
	Over On The Sunny Side (Al Bowlly)	21 Feb 1934	HMV B6463	(128)
	You Have Taken My Heart (Al Bowlly)	5 Apr 1934	HMV B6477	(128)
	You Oughta Be In Pictures (Al Bowlly)	5 Apr 1934	HMV B6477	(128 138)
	She Loves Me Not (Al Bowlly)	27 Apr 1934	HMV B6485	(129 C12)
	Fair And Warmer (Al Bowlly)	28 Jun 1934	HMV B6503	(129 C14)
	Happy! (Al Bowlly)	6 Jul 1934	HMV B6507	(129)
	All I Do Is Dream Of You (Al Bowlly)	11 Jul 1934	HMV B6508	(130 136 C85) C153
	Freckle Face, You're Beautiful (Al Bowlly)	24 Aug 1934	HMV B6512	(130)

Produced & Transferred by John Wadley   Sleeve Note by Brian Rust

Titles contained in Collections only:

	THE NIGHT CLUB KINGS (Directed By RAY NOBLE):			
C148	Someone (Pat O'Malley)	21 Jan 1930	HMV B5776	(C70)
	In The Moonlight (Pat O'Malley)	21 Jan 1930	HMV B5776	(C70)
	NEW MAYFAIR DANCE ORCHESTRA:			
C153	Time On My Hands (Al Bowlly)	19 Feb 1931	HMV B5983	(118 131 135 C17 C93)
	RAY NOBLE AND HIS NEW MAYFAIR DANCE ORCHESTRA:			
	Looking On The Bright Side Of Life (Al Bowlly)	1 Sep 1932	HMV B6237	(122 133)
	RAY NOBLE AND HIS ORCHESTRA:			
	Please (Al Bowlly)	8 Dec 1932	HMV B6283	(123)
	A Little Street Where Old Friends Meet (Al Bowlly)	12 Jan 1933	HMV B6305	(123)
	Have You Ever Been Lonely? (Al Bowlly)	7 Feb 1933	HMV B6319	(124 136 C24 C84)
	The Moment I Saw You (Al Bowlly)	27 Feb 1933	HMV B6325	(124 137)
	The Old Spinning Wheel (Al Bowlly)	10 May 1933	HMV B6348	(125)
	Thanks (Al Bowlly)	27 Oct 1933	HMV B6413	(127 143)
	My Song Goes Round The World (Al Bowlly)	7 Dec 1933	HMV B6438	(127 143)
	Did You Ever See A Dream Walking? (Al Bowlly)	20 Dec 1933	HMV B6441	(127 143 C85 C93)
	I Love You Truly (Al Bowlly)	31 May 1934	HMV B6492	(129 C23)
	NOVELTY ORCHESTRA:			
	You're Driving Me Crazy (Al Bowlly)	19 Feb 1931	HMV B3775	(118 138 C93)
	NEW MAYFAIR DANCE ORCHESTRA:			
C154	Blaze Away (Unknown)	25 Aug 1931	HMV B6057	
	RAY NOBLE AND HIS ORCHESTRA:			
	Wheezy Anna (Al Bowlly & Chorus)	7 Feb 1933	HMV B6316	(124)
	All Over Italy (They Sing So Prettily) (Al Bowlly & Chorus)	24 May 1933	HMV B6364	(125)
C156	Experiment (Al Bowlly)	12 Oct 1933	HMV B6408	(126 134 143 C10)
	NEW MAYFAIR DANCE ORCHESTRA:			
C163	Any Time's The Time To Fall In Love (Jack Plant)	20 Jun 1930	HMV B5856	(C121)

(1)	(2)	(3)	(4)	(5)

THE ORGAN, THE DANCE BAND AND ME

See under BILLY THORBURN

JACK PAYNE

(b 22 August 1899; d 4 December 1969)

(1)	(2)	(3)	(4)	(5)
222	JACK PAYNE - Rhythmatitis : EMI Retrospect Series SH 508			
	HOTEL CECIL DANCE ORCHESTRA (Directed By JACK PAYNE):			
	Yes Sir! That's My Baby (N/V)	27 Aug 1925	Zon 2634	
	Sally's Come Back (N/V)	27 Aug 1925	Zon 2635	
	JACK PAYNE AND HIS BBC DANCE ORCHESTRA:			
	Out Of The Dawn (Jack Payne)	2 Oct 1928	Col 5074	
	Sweet Sue, Just You (Trio of Jack Payne, Bob Busby & Bob Manning)	2 Oct 1928	Col 5074	(146)
	A Dicky Bird Told Me So (Trio as previously)	21 Mar 1929	Col 5360	(146)
	I Faw Down And Go Boom (Trio as previously)	16 Apr 1929	Col 5360	C154
	Blondy (Jack Payne)	1 Mar 1930	Col CB28	
	When It's Springtime In The Rockies (Jack Payne & Jack Plant)	28 Jun 1930	Col CB106	
	The Moochi (Jack Payne)	26 Sep 1930	Col CB142	
	My Baby Just Cares For Me (Trio as previously)	15 Oct 1930	Col CB154	(146) C163
	If I Could Be With You One Hour Tonight (Val Rosing)	15 Oct 1930	Col CB155	(146)
	Lady Of Spain (Val Rosing)	3 Mar 1931	Col CB242	
	River, Stay 'Way From My Door (Jack Payne)	17 Mar 1931	Col CB254	
	Miss Elizabeth Brown (Jack Payne)	24 Mar 1931	Col CB254	
	Lazy Day (Jack Payne)	19 Jun 1931	Col CB312	(145)
	When The Moon Comes Over The Mountain (Trio as previously)	19 Jun 1931	Col CB312	
	Rhythmatitis (Jack Payne & Billy Scott-Coomber)	26 Oct 1931	Reg MR496	
	Guilty (Billy Scott-Coomber)	21 Nov 1931	Col CB386	
	Love Letters In The Sand (Jack Payne)	4 Dec 1931	Reg MR495	
	JACK PAYNE AND HIS BAND:			
	Hot Coffee (Billy Scott-Coomber)	c 10 Mar 1932	Imp 2677	

Produced, Compiled & Transferred by Chris Ellis — Sleeve Note by Brian Rust

Titles contained in Collections only:

(1)	(2)	(3)	(4)	(5)
	JACK PAYNE AND HIS BAND:			
C146	It's A Lovely Day Tomorrow (Billy Scott-Coomber)	14 Feb 1940	Dec F7403	C176
	JACK PAYNE AND HIS BBC DANCE ORCHESTRA:			
C154	Airman! Airman! (Jack Payne & Chorus)	21 Mar 1930	Col DB93	
	Sing Holly, Go Whistle, Hey! Hey! (Trio of Jack Payne, Bob Busby & Bob Manning)	17 Feb 1931	Col CB232	
	JACK PAYNE AND HIS BAND:			
	Let's All Sing Like The Birdies Sing (Leslie Holmes)	Nov/Dec 1932	Imp 2801	
	JACK PAYNE AND HIS BBC DANCE ORCHESTRA:			
C155	Love For Sale (N/V)	27 Jun 1931	Col CB318	

(1)	(2)	(3)	(4)	(5)

ROLAND PEACHEY
(b 1912)

	ROLAND PEACHEY AND HIS ROYAL HAWAIIANS:			
C174	I Got Rhythm (N/V)	4 Feb 1944	Dec F8799	

SID PHILLIPS
(b 14 June 1907; d 25 May 1973)

	SID PHILLIPS' QUINTET:			
C142	Royal Garden Blues (N/V)	6 May 1941	Dec F7972	(C45)
	(Note: Recording date amended from that shown in Catalogue)			
C143	Strut Miss Lizzie (N/V)	27 Nov 1940	Dec F7758	
C174	Ridin' High (The Greene Sisters)	14 Jan 1941	Dec F7723	

PICCADILLY PLAYERS

	Directed by AL STARITA:			
C148	Kiss And Make Up (Eddie Grossbart)	20 Apr 1928	Col 4907	(C29)

DANNY POLO
(b 1901; d 11 July 1949)

	DANNY POLO AND HIS SWING STARS:			
C143	Stratton Street Strut (N/V)	1 Oct 1937	Dec F6518	(C45 C72)

LOU PREAGER
(b 12 January 1906; d 14 November 1978)

	LOU PREAGER AND HIS ORCHESTRA:			
C176	Cruising Down The River (Paul Rich)	7 Dec 1945	Col FB3180	(C48)

OSCAR RABIN
(b 26 April 1899; d 20 June 1958)

	OSCAR RABIN AND HIS BAND:			
C169	An Apple For The Teacher (Beryl Davis & Garry Gowan)	8 Nov 1939	Rex 9671	
	A Man And His Dream (Garry Gowan)	8 Nov 1939	Rex 9671	
	Moonlight Avenue (Diane)	8 Apr 1940	Rex 9768	
	When The Rose Of Tralee Met Danny Boy (Beryl Davis)	8 Apr 1940	Rex 9768	
	When Night Is Thru' (Bob Dale)	18 Dec 1941	Rex 10090	
	Sometimes (Diane)	24 Apr 1942	Dec F8124	
	You're Mine (Diane)	29 May 1942	Dec F8143	
	Basin Street Ball (Terry Devon & Benny Lee)	3 Jul 1942	Dec F8164	
	Sing, Everybody, Sing (Terry Devon, Beryl Davis, Diane & the Boys)	3 Jul 1942	Dec F8164	
C174	My Wubba Dolly (Beryl Davis & Billy Nicholls)	20 Feb 1940	Rex 9742	
	OSCAR RABIN AND HIS STRICT TEMPO DANCE BAND:			
	Dancing Time (N/V)	23 Jan 1941	Dec F7737	

THE RHYTHMIC EIGHT

See under BERT FIRMAN

THE RHYTHM MANIACS

See under PHILIP LEWIS

EDMUNDO ROS
(b 7 December 1910)

223 EDMUNDO ROS AND HIS RUMBA BAND - Cuban Love Song : Decca DVL 9

Cuban Love Song (N/V)	Oct 1946	Dec F8725	
The Coffee Song (Edmundo Ros)	May 1947	Dec F8800	C146
Rio De Janeiro (Edmundo Ros)	Mar 1945	Dec F8869	
The Wedding Samba (Edmundo Ros)	Aug 1949	Dec F9200	
Manana (Is Soon Enough For Me) (Edmundo Ros & Band)	Jun 1947	Dec F8882	(154) C146
Big Brass Band From Brazil (Edmundo Ros)	May 1948	Dec F8923	
Managua Nicaragua (Edmundo Ros)	Jun 1947	Dec F8815	
Take It Away (Edmundo Ros)	Apr 1946	Dec F8630	
South America Take It Away (Edmundo Ros)	Jun 1947	Dec F8815	
Come With Me My Honey (Edmundo Ros)	Sep 1944	Dec F8508	(154)
Maria From Bahia (Edmundo Ros)	Sep 1948	Dec F9012	
I'm Crazy For You (Edmundo Ros)	Jun 1946	Dec F8665	
I Got The Sun In The Morning (N/V)	May 1947	Dec F8800	
The Mararajah Of Magador (Edmundo Ros)	Feb 1949	Dec F9108	
Come Closer To Me (Ronaldo Mazar)	Jun 1946	Dec F8681	
The Three Caballeros (Ronaldo Mazar, Johnnie & Edmundo Ros)	Mar 1945	Dec F8459	
Her Bathing Suit Never Got Wet (Edmundo Ros)	Oct 1946	Dec F8708	

Note: The remaining track in this album, "It Was Never Like This", was recorded in June 1953.

Compiled & Remastered by Colin Brown — Sleeve Note by Gary Bailey

Titles contained in Collections only:

C174	Quien No Llora No Mama (Edmundo Ros)	10 Jan 1947	Dec F8841

HARRY ROY
(b 12 January 1900; d 1 February 1971)

224 HARRY ROY AND HIS ORCHESTRA - Truckin' On Down, : Old Bean Records OLD 8

Truckin' On Down (Harry Roy)	14 Oct 1935	Par F304	
No Moon, No Stars, Just You (Ivor Moreton)	6 Feb 1935	Par F124	
London On A Rainy Night (Ivor Moreton)	4 Jan 1935	Par F103	
Troublesome Trumpet (Harry Roy & Chorus)	6 May 1934	Par R1857	C164
Smoke Gets In Your Eyes (Ivor Moreton)	31 Oct 1934	Par R1969	
The Beat O' My Heart (Bill Currie)	6 May 1934	Par R1857	(157)

(1)	(2)	(3)	(4)	(5)
	Gertie, The Girl With The Gong (Bill Currie & Ivor Moreton)	19 Mar 1935	Par F143	
	The Object Of My Affection (Bill Currie)	18 Feb 1935	Par F126	
	Cowboy In Manhattan (N/V)	23 Jul 1935	Par F223	
	Let's Have A Jubilee (Bill Currie & Chorus)	26 Feb 1935	Par F129	
	Louisiana Lullaby (Harry Roy)	23 Nov 1933	Par R1710	(157)
	We're Gonna Have Smooth Sailing (Harry Roy)	2 Jul 1935	Par F189	
	Love And A Dime (Harry Roy)	23 Jul 1935	Par F223	
	The Words Are In My Heart (N/V)	22 May 1935	Par F174	
	My Hat's On The Side Of My Head (Harry Roy)	23 Nov 1933	Par R1710	
	I Was In The Mood (Harry Roy & Bill Currie)	12 Oct 1933	Par R1671	
	Hurricane Harry (Bill Carrie)	7 Jun 1933	Par R1553	
	Stars Over Devon (Ivor Moreton)	14 Oct 1935	Par F304	
	You've Got Me Crying Again (Ivor Moreton)	8 May 1933	Par R1521	
	Swingy Little Thingy (Harry Roy)	12 Oct 1933	Par R1672	

Produced & Transferred by Colin Brown   Sleeve Note by Freddy Clayton

225 HARRY ROY, HIS TIGER-RAGAMUFFINS AND ORCHESTRA-
Everybody's Swinging It Now : Living Era AJA 5050

(1)	(2)	(3)	(4)	(5)
	HARRY ROY'S TIGER RAGAMUFFINS With Clarinet & Vocal By Harry Roy:			
	Jazz Me Blues (Harry Roy)	15 Apr 1936	Par F458	
	HARRY ROY AND HIS ORCHESTRA:			
	You Gotta Know How To Dance (Bill Currie)	29 Jun 1936	Par F501	
	HARRY ROY'S TIGER-RAGAMUFFINS With Clarinet & Vocal By Harry Roy:			
	Someday Sweetheart (Harry Roy)	9 Jun 1936	Par F484	
	Cheerful Blues (Harry Roy)	15 Apr 1936	Par F458	(158)
	HARRY ROY AND HIS ORCHESTRA:			
	Everybody's Swinging It Now (Harry Roy)	29 Jun 1936	Par F502	
	HARRY ROY'S TIGER-RAGAMUFFINS Featuring Clarinet & Vocal By Harry Roy:			
	Hot Lips (Harry Roy)	3 Dec 1936	Par F624	
	HARRY ROY'S TIGER-RAGAMUFFINS:			
	Fox-Trot Medley, Part 1 (N/V) - Jealous / Whispering / Poor Butterfly	31 Oct 1934	Par R1970	
	HARRY ROY AND HIS ORCHESTRA:			
	Every Time I Look At You (Harry Roy)	29 Jun 1936	Par F502	
	The Scat Singers (Trio of Harry Roy, Bill Currie & Abe Romaine)	13 Jul 1936	Par F539	
	Swing (Dinah Miller & Harry Roy)	25 Feb 1936	Par F409	
	HARRY ROY'S TIGER-RAGAMUFFINS:			
	Medley - Farewell Blues (N/V) / You Rascal, You (Harry Roy) / Muddy Water (N/V)	Jan 1934	Par R1771	
	HARRY ROY AND HIS ORCHESTRA:			
	Shine (Harry Roy)	9 Jun 1936	Par F500	
	HARRY ROY'S TIGER-RAGAMUFFINS:			
	That's A-Plenty (N/V)	9 Jun 1936	Par F484	
	Medley (N/V) - Memories Of You / Rain / Goodbye Blues	6 May 1934	Par R1859	

(1)	(2)	(3)	(4)	(5)
	HARRY ROY AND HIS ORCHESTRA:			
	Eeny Meeny Miney Mo (Dinah Miller & Harry Roy)	25 Feb 1936	Par F409	
	HARRY ROY'S TIGER-RAGAMUFFINS Featuring Clarinet & Vocal By Harry Roy:			
	I'm A Ding Dong Daddy (Harry Roy)	3 Dec 1936	Par F624	
	HARRY ROY AND HIS ORCHESTRA (recorded at Empire Theatre, Leeds):			
	Harry Roy Stage Show, Part 1 -	c 8 Oct 1936	Par F609	
	Bugle Call Rag (From Par R1526)			
	Tiger Rag			
	Knock Knock (Band)			
	Alone (Audience)			
	Harry Roy Stage Show, Part 2 -	c 8 Oct 1936	Par F609	
	Sarawaki			(162)
	St. Louis Blues			
	Piano Madness			
	Somebody Stole My Gal			(162)

Produced & Remastered by Colin Brown   Sleeve Note by John Tracy

Titles contained in Collections only:

(1)	(2)	(3)	(4)	(5)
	HARRY ROY AND HIS ORCHESTRA:			
C156	Night And Day (Diana Clare)	Aug 1933	Par R1646	(C10)
	Miss Otis Regrets (Trio of Harry Roy, Bill Currie & Ivor Moreton)	Aug 1934	Par R1919	(C10)
	I Get A Kick Out Of You (Bill Currie)	24 May 1935	Par F176	(C10)
	HARRY ROY AND HIS BAND:			
	Let's Be Buddies (Harry Roy & Chorus)	30 May 1941	RZ MR3493	(C10)
	HARRY ROY AND HIS ORCHESTRA:			
C163	Like Taking Candy From A Baby (Harry Roy)	Jul 1934	Par R1884	(157)
	Say It (Ivor Moreton)	Sep 1934	Par R1939	(157)
C164	Canadian Capers (Ensemble)	Apr 1933	Par R1505	(156 159)
	Bugle Call Rag (N/V)	May 1933	Par R1526	(156 159)
	Twelfth Street Rag (N/V)	Jun 1933	Par R1568	(156 159 160)
	Lover (Leslie Hutchinson)*	Jun 1933	Par R1595	(C110 C124)
	Let's Call It A Day (Leslie Hutchinson)*	Jun 1933	Par R1595	(C124)
	There's A New Day Comin' (Harry Roy)	Jul-Aug 1933	Par R1584	(157)
	Eadie Was A Lady (Harry Roy & Chorus)	Nov 1933	Par R1709	
	Black Panther (N/V)	Nov 1933	Par R1677	
	Build A Little Home (Ivor Moreton)	Mar 1934	Par R1795	(157 C17)
	Mama Don't Want No Peas And Rice And Coconut Oil (Trio of Harry Roy, Bill Currie & Ivor Moreton)	Apr 1934	Par R1812	
	The Roy Rag (N/V)	24 Jul 1934	Par R1896	(156 159)
	When A St. Louis Woman Comes Down To New Orleans (Harry Roy)	31 Oct 1934	Par R1969	(162)
	Rock And Roll (Harry Roy)	Dec 1934	Par R2012	(157)
	(* Original issues as Leslie Hutchinson accompanied by Harry Roy and His Orchestra)			
C167	Leicester Square Rag (Johnny Green & Band)	4 Oct 1949	Par F2387	(162)
C174	Sambina (N/V)	17 Apr 1947	Dec Unissued take (F8896)	
	The Darktown Strutters' Ball (Harry Roy & The Keynotes)	23 Mar 1948	Dec F8924	(164 165)

(1)	(2)	(3)	(4)	(5)

SYD ROY
(b 31 December 1895; d 17 November 1981)

	SYD ROY'S LYRICALS:			
C164	Stay Out Of The South (Eddie Collis)	1 Jun 1928	Imp 1906	
	My Pet (Eddie Collis)	6 Jul 1928	Imp 1921	

ROYAL AIR FORCE DANCE ORCHESTRA/SQUADRONAIRES

	THE SQUADRONAIRES:			
C146	Cement Mixer (The Quads)	27 Jun 1946	Dec F8644	(C107)
	Five Minutes More (Jimmy Miller & The Quads)	17 Dec 1946	Dec F8747	(174)
	The Wishing Waltz (Sam Browne)*	5 Mar 1948	Dec F8862	
C168	You're Driving Me Crazy (The Quads)	20 Apr 1948	Dec F8927	
	THE ROYAL AIR FORCE DANCE ORCHESTRA:			
C169	It's Foolish But It's Fun (Sid Colin)	19 May 1941	Dec F7861	
	There I Go (Jimmy Miller)	19 May 1941	Dec F7862	
	You Started Something (Jimmy Miller)	2 Oct 1941	Dec F7994	
	Blue Champagne (Jimmy Miller)	13 Nov 1941	Dec F8020	
	The Whistler's Mother-In-Law (Sid Colin)	13 Mar 1942	Dec F8111	
	Keep An Eye On Your Heart (Sid Colin)	19 May 1943	Dec F8319	(C104)
	Lover's Lullaby (Jimmy Miller)	19 May 1943	Dec F8319	
	All Our Tomorrows (Jimmy Miller)	19 May 1943	Dec F8315	
	Out Of Nowhere (Dorothy Carless)	17 Oct 1945	Dec F8575	(C104)
	THE SQUADRONAIRES:			
C172	Reflections On The Water (Sam Browne)*	5 Mar 1948	Dec F8881	

(*Original issues as Sam Browne with the Squadronaires)

SAVOY HAVANA BAND

C178	Why Did I Kiss That Girl? (Cyril Ramon Newton)	Apr 1924	Col 3440	

SAVOY ORPHEANS

226 SAVOY ORPHEANS - Stomp Off, Let's Go : Halcyon HDL 111

	Eccentric (N/V)	19 Apr 1924	Col 3432	(C49 C56)
	Oh! Eva (Ain't You Coming Out Tonight?) (N/V)	18 Aug 1924	Col 3494	(C56)
	Hard Hearted Hannah (N/V)	21 Jan 1925	HMV B1955	(C56)
	Copenhagen (N/V)	21 Jan 1925	HMV B1954	(C56)
	Come On Over (N/V)	3 Mar 1925	HMV B1987	
	Blue Evening Blues (N/V)	4 May 1925	HMV B2035	(C56)
	Oh! That Sweet In Suite 16 (N/V)	16 Jul 1925	HMV B2102	(C56)
	Stomp Off, Let's Go (N/V)	23 Oct 1925	HMV B2174	
	Dinah (N/V)	30 Oct 1925	HMV B2183	(C56)
	Static Strut (N/V)	4 Jun 1926	HMV B5083	
	Jig Walk (Chorus by Band)	6 Oct 1926	HMV B5136	
	Hop Skip (N/V)	22 Dec 1926	HMV B5198	
	I'm Telling The Birds (N/V)	28 Jan 1927	HMV B5214	
	Back Beats (N/V)	23 Feb 1927	HMV B5226	
	Little Brown Baby (N/V)	1 Jul 1927	HMV B5310	
	Vladivostock (N/V)	15 Jul 1927	HMV B5373	(C56)
	Ain't That Too Bad? (N/V)	15 Jul 1927	HMV B5342	(C56)

(1)	(2)	(3)	(4)	(5)
	That's My Hap-Hap-Happiness (N/V)	18 Jul 1927	HMV B5310	

Produced & Transferred by John Wadley & John R. Bennett   Sleeve Note by Brian Rust

Titles contained in Collections only:

(1)	(2)	(3)	(4)	(5)
	SAVOY ORPHEANS:			
C158	The Blue Room (The Hamilton Sisters & Fordyce)	1 Jul 1927	HMV B5322	
C163	Baby Face (Cyril Ramon Newton) & another)	13 Oct 1926	HMV B5147	(C56 C137)

PRIMO SCALA

See under HARRY BIDGOOD

GEORGE SCOTT-WOOD
(b 27 May 1903; d 28 October 1978)

(1)	(2)	(3)	(4)	(5)
	GEORGE SCOTT WOOD AND HIS ORCHESTRA Accompanying Larry Adler (Harmonica):			
C166	Stormy Weather	29 Jan 1938	Col FB1911	

GEORGE SHEARING
(b 13 August 1919)

(1)	(2)	(3)	(4)	(5)
	GEORGE SHEARING QUARTET:			
C142	Afraid Of You (N/V)	22 Jun 1944	Dec Unissued	(169)

VICTOR SILVESTER
(b 25 February 1900; d 14 August 1978)

227 VICTOR SILVESTER AND HIS BALLROOM ORCHESTRA/VICTOR SILVESTER'S JIVE BAND - Get Rhythm In Your Feet : EMI Retrospect Series EG 26 0627 1

(1)	(2)	(3)	(4)	(5)
	VICTOR SILVESTER AND HIS BALLROOM ORCHESTRA:			
	Get Rhythm In Your Feet (N/V)	1 Apr 1936	Par F448	
	The Lambeth Walk/Did You Go Down Lambeth Way? (N/V)	4 May 1938/ 7 Feb 1939	Par F1115/ F1357	
	Little Lady Make Believe (N/V)	30 Sep 1938	Par F1234	
	Music, Maestro Please (N/V)	30 Sep 1938	Par F1234	
	Florianopolis (N/V)	23 Nov 1938	Par F1290	
	I Shall Always Remember You Smiling	10 Feb 1939	Par F1357	
	VICTOR SILVESTER'S JIVE BAND: (N/V)			
	Why Do I Lie To Myself About You (N/V)	2 May 1945	Col FB3153	
	Straighten Up And Fly Right (N/V)	2 May 1945	Col FB3217	
	VICTOR SILVESTER AND HIS BALLROOM ORCHESTRA:			
	Moonlight Avenue (N/V)	29 Feb 1940	Par F1673	
	Don't Ever Pass Me By (N/V)	7 May 1940	Par F1735	
	Begin The Beguine (N/V)	14 Jun 1940	Par F1745	
	On The Sunny Side Of The Street (N/V)	4 Nov 1940	Col FB2528	
	I'll Pray For You (N/V)	1 Dec 1939	Par F1606	
	How Deep Is The Ocean? (N/V)	Aug 1947	Col FB3328	
	I Hum A Waltz (N/V)	8 Oct 1937	Par F920	
	South Of Pago Pago (N/V)	Aug 1949	Col FB3519	

(1)	(2)	(3)	(4)	(5)
	VICTOR SILVESTER'S JIVE BAND:			
	Sweet Georgia Brown (N/V)	2 May 1945	Col FB3153	
	Ac-Cent-Tchu-Ate The Positive (N/V)	2 May 1945	Col FB3217	
	VICTOR SILVESTER AND HIS BALLROOM ORCHESTRA:			
	If I Should Fall In Love Again (N/V)	14 Jun 1940	Par F1745	
	Don't Say Goodbye (N/V)	8 Oct 1937	Par F920	

Produced, Compiled & Transferred by Chris Ellis — Sleeve Note by Geoff Williams

228 VICTOR SILVESTER'S JIVE BAND Featuring George Chisholm and Tommy McQuater : EMI Retrospect Series EG 26 0580 1

(1)	(2)	(3)	(4)	(5)
	Stomping At The Savoy (N/V)	13 Nov 1943	Col FB2980	
	Way Down Yonder In New Orleans (N/V)	13 Nov 1943	Col FB2980	
	Pardon Me, Pretty Baby (N/V)	18 Dec 1943	Col FB2989	
	Crazy Rhythm (N/V)	18 Dec 1943	Col FB2989	
	I'm Coming, Virginia (N/V)	14 Jan 1944	Col FB2996	
	Poor Butterfly (N/V)	14 Jan 1944	Col FB2996	
	I Wish I Were Twins (N/V)	12 Feb 1944	Col FB3004	
	You Took Advantage Of Me (N/V)	12 Feb 1944	Col FB3004	
	How Am I To Know? (N/V)	17 Feb 1944	Col FB3008	
	Ida, Sweet As Apple Cider (N/V)	17 Feb 1944	Col FB3008	
	Blue Lou (N/V)	27 Mar 1944	Col FB3019	
	Please Do It Again (N/V)	27 Mar 1944	Col FB3019	
	My Melancholy Baby (N/V)	7 Apr 1944	Col FB3027	
	How Come You Do Me Like You Do? (N/V)	7 Apr 1944	Col FB3027	
	The One I Love Belongs To Somebody Else (N/V)	20 Apr 1944	Col FB3044	
	Love Me, Or Leave (N/V)	20 Apr 1944	Col FB3044	
	Undecided (N/V)	14 Nov 1944	Col FB3072	
	Boston Bounce (N/V)	14 Nov 1944	Col FB3072	(C41)
	There's Honey On The Moon Tonight (N/V)	14 Nov 1944	Col FB3085	(C71)
	Coquette (comp J.Green, G.Kahn, C.Lombardo) (N/V)	14 Nov 1944	Col FB3085	

Produced, Compiled & Transferred by Chris Ellis — Sleeve Note by Tony Middleton

DEBROY SOMERS
(b 11 April 1890; d 27 May 1952)

(1)	(2)	(3)	(4)	(5)
	DEBROY SOMERS' BAND:			
C154	I'm Going Back To Himazaz (Fred Austin)	2 Sep 1927	Col 4506	

THE SQUADRONAIRES

See under ROYAL AIR FORCE DANCE ORCHESTRA

RAY STARITA
(b c 1900; d 1967)

(1)	(2)	(3)	(4)	(5)
	RAY STARITA AND HIS AMBASSADORS CLUB BAND:			
C148	Rhapsody In Rhythm (N/V)	30 Jun 1928	Col 5008	(175)
C163	Crazy Rhythm (Trio including Eddie Grossbart)	29 Sep 1928	Col 5137	(175)
	RAY STARITA AND HIS AMBASSADORS:			
C174	The Old Man Of The Mountain (Sam Browne)	Sep 1932	Ster 1050	

LEW STONE
(b 28 May 1898; d 13 February 1969)

229 LEW STONE AND HIS BAND Featuring Al Bowlly - Right From The Heart
Old Bean Records OLD 3

LEW STONE AND THE MONSEIGNEUR BAND:			
Rain, Rain, Go Away (Al Bowlly)	31 Oct 1932	Dec F3233	(178)
Why Waste Your Tears? (Al Bowlly)	31 Oct 1932	Dec F3233	
I Can't Write The Words (Al Bowlly)	16 Nov 1932	Dec F3270	
Someone To Care For (Al Bowlly)	2 Mar 1933	Dec F3502	
Three Wishes (Al Bowlly)	5 Apr 1933	Dec F3534	
I Lay Me Down To Sleep (Al Bowlly)	7 Jun 1933	Dec F3603	
In The Park In Paree (Al Bowlly)	7 Jun 1933	Dec F3592	(C88)
The Language Of Love (Al Bowlly)	7 Jun 1933	Dec F3603	
Isn't It Heavenly? (Al Bowlly)	1 Aug 1933	Dec F3630	(180 C22)
LEW STONE AND HIS BAND:			
Don't Change (Al Bowlly)	24 Oct 1933	Dec F3821	
The Day You Came Along (Al Bowlly)	24 Oct 1933	Dec F3722	(178)
Thanks (Al Bowlly)	24 Oct 1933	Dec F3722	(178 C88)
Eadie Was A Lady (Al Bowlly & Band)	29 Dec 1933	Dec F3825	(179)
Gosh, I Must Be Falling In Love (Al Bowlly)	15 Feb 1934	Dec F3884	
What Is There To Take Its Place? (Al Bowlly)	25 Apr 1934	Dec F5003	
I Love You Truly (Al Bowlly)	3 May 1934	Dec F5003	(180 C22)
As Long As I Live (Al Bowlly)	3 Aug 1934	Dec F5132	(181)
Straight From The Shoulder (Al Bowlly)	3 Aug 1934	Dec F5158	(C83)

Produced & Transferred by John Wadley   Sleeve Note by Austin Clegg

230 The Golden Age Of LEW STONE AND HIS ORCHESTRA : EMI GX 41 2534 1

Stay As Sweet As You Are (Alan Kane)	28 Dec 1934	RZ MR1558	(185)
Solitude (N/V)	28 Dec 1934	RZ MR1561	(185)
Sidewalks Of Cuba (Joe Crossman)	11 Feb 1935	RZ MR1583	(185)
My Old Dog (Nat Gonella)	25 Feb 1935	RZ MR1629	(185)
Two Trumpet Toot (Tiny Winters & Band)	25 Feb 1935	RZ MR1629	(185)
It's Easy To Remember (Alan Kane)	14 Mar 1935	RZ MR1627	(185)
Dust Off That Old Pianna (Alfie Noakes)	14 Mar 1935	RZ MR1628	(185)
Yes Suh! (Joe Crossman)	30 Mar 1935	RZ MR1678	(185)
The Bouncing Ball (N/V)	30 Mar 1935	RZ MR1678	(185)
The Gentleman Obviously Doesn't Believe In Love (Lew Stone)	10 Apr 1935	RZ MR1672	(185)
Here Comes Cookie (Tiny Winters)	10 Apr 1935	RZ MR1673	(185)
Where Were You On The Night Of June The Third? (Tiny Winters)	10 Apr 1935	RZ MR1673	(185)
The Girl With The Dreamy Eyes (Tiny Winters)	10 Apr 1935	RZ MR1677	(185)
Zing! Went The Strings Of My Heart (Joe Crossman & Trio of Alfie Noakes, Joe Ferrie & Don Barrigo)	4 May 1935	RZ MR1708	(185 C20)
I Won't Dance (Al Hoffman & The Radio Three: Kay Cavendish, Joy Worth & Ann Carring)	18 Jul 1935	RZ MR1785	(185)
East Of The Sun (Joe Ferrie)	12 Oct 1935	RZ MR1872	(185)

Produced by Chris Ellis
Transferred by John Wadley

(1)	(2)	(3)	(4)	(5)
	Titles contained in Collections only:			
	LEW STONE AND HIS BAND:			
C142	White Jazz (N/V)	3 Nov 1933	Dec F3782	(179 184 C43 C81)
	LEW STONE AND HIS NOVA-TONES:			
C146	Let It Snow, Let It Snow, Let It Snow (Ronnie O'Dell)	18 Feb 1946	Dec F8614	(183)
	LEW STONE AND HIS BAND:			
C157	Hand In Hand (Al Bowlly)	3 May 1934	Dec F3985	(180)
C169	A Mother's Prayer At Twilight (Sam Browne)	13 Nov 1939	Dec F7294	
	We'll Meet Again (Sam Browne)	13 Nov 1939	Dec F7294	
	It's A Blue World (Sam Browne)	10 May 1940	Dec F7490	
	In A Little Rocky Valley (Sam Browne)	10 May 1940	Dec F7489	
	Sing A Round-Up Song (Sam Browne)	10 May 1940	Dec F7489	
	Too Romantic (Wendy Claire)	10 May 1940	Dec F7490	
	And So Do I (Sam Browne)	10 Dec 1940	Dec F7690	
	The Hut-Sut Song (Carl Barriteau & Chorus)	4 Jul 1941	Dec F7919	(C105)
	There's Nothing New To Tell You (Rita Carr)	12 Oct 1942	Dec F8215	
	LEW STONE AND THE MONSEIGNEUR BAND:			
C174	My Heart's To Let (Al Bowlly)	2 Mar 1933	Dec F3496	
	LEW STONE AND HIS STONECRACKERS:			
	Get Happy (N/V)	21 May 1941	Dec Unissued	(183)
	LEW STONE AND HIS NOVA-TONES:			
	I'll Buy That Dream (Helen Mack & Ronnie O'Dell)	18 Feb 1946	Dec F8615	(C104)
	LEW STONE AND HIS BAND:			
C175	I Hear A Rhapsody (Benny Lee)	4 Jul 1941	Dec F7919	
	Number Ten Lullaby Lane (Benny Lee)	4 Jul 1941	Dec F7920	
	When They Sound The Last 'All Clear' (Benny Lee)	13 Sep 1941	Dec F7978	
	As If You Didn't Know (Benny Lee)	12 Nov 1941	Dec F8032	
	Why Don't We Do This More Often? (Benny Lee)	12 Nov 1941	Dec F8032	
	I Guess I'll Have To Dream The Rest (Benny Lee)	12 Nov 1941	Dec F8033	
	Lonely Serenade (Benny Lee)	12 Nov 1941	Dec F8033	
	We Both Told A Lie (Benny Lee)	17 Nov 1941	Dec F8056	
	What More Can I Say? (Benny Lee)	20 Jan 1942	Dec F8083	
C176	I Get Along Without You Very Well (Sam Browne)	15 Aug 1939	Dec F7171	(178)
C179	How Could We Be Wrong? (Al Bowlly)	3 Nov 1933	Dec F3734	(180)

NAT TEMPLE

(1)	(2)	(3)	(4)	(5)
	NAT TEMPLE AND HIS CLUB ROYAL ORCHESTRA:			
C174	Nattering Around (N/V)	23 Apr 1945	Dec F8611	(C125)

BILLY TERNENT

(b 10 October 1899; d 23 March 1977)

(1)	(2)	(3)	(4)	(5)
	BILLY TERNENT AND HIS ORCHESTRA:			
C172	I Like Riding On A Choo Choo (Leslie Sarony)	Mar 1949	Dec F9122	(186)

BILLY THORNBURN
(b 12 May 1900; d 4 April 1971)

231 BILLY THORBURN'S 'THE ORGAN, THE DANCE BAND & ME' Featuring Robinson Cleaver - Let's Break The Good News : EMI Retrospect Series SH 504

(1)	(2)	(3)	(4)	(5)
	Let's Break The Good News (Helen Raymond)	3 Nov 1938	Par F1291	
	With The Wind And The Rain In Your Hair (George Barclay)	3 Apr 1940	Par F1709	
	Wish Me Luck (As You Wave Me Goodbye) (Terry Devon)	28 Jul 1939	Par F1511	
	I'd Never, Never, Fall In Love Again (Kay Harding)	16 Dec 1941	Par F1887	
	All Over The Place (Alan Kane)	10 Oct 1940	Par F1784	
	All Along With My Shadow (Helen Clare)	22 Aug 1941	Par F1858	
	*The Mem'ry Of A Rose (Chick Henderson)	5 Sep 1940	Par F1770	
	Love Makes The World Go Round (Helen Raymond)	3 Nov 1938	Par F1291	
	It's Foolish But It's Fun (Terry Devon)	3 May 1941	Par F1838	
	Faithful Forever (George Barclay)	2 Jan 1940	Par F1635	
	If I Could Paint A Memory (Julie Dawn)	17 Jan 1942	Par F1903	
	*There'll Come Another Day (Chick Henderson)	5 Sep 1940	Par F1787	(187)
	I Spy (Alan Kane)	6 Apr 1943	Par F1979	
	You're So Sweet To Remember (Primrose Orrock)	7 Apr 1945	Par F2089	
	**Too Many Irons In The Fire (Harry Kaye)	2 Oct 1946	Par F2190	
	**I'm Happy For Your Sake (Rita Williams)	2 Oct 1946	Par F2198	

*Un-named Compton organist **Andrew Fenner (Compton organ)

Compiled by Hugh Palmer Sleeve Note by Hugh Palmer

MADAME TUSSAUD'S DANCE ORCHESTRA

See under STANLEY BARNETT

VALAIDA (SNOW)
(b c1900; d 30 May 1956)

VALAIDA (Trumpet & Vocal) Accomp by BILLY MASON AND HIS ORCHESTRA:

(1)	(2)	(3)	(4)	(5)
C147	I Can't Dance (I Got Ants In My Pants)	19 Jan 1935	Par F118	(188)

VALIDA (Trumpet & Vocal) With Swing Accomp directed by GEORGE SCOTT-WOOD:

(1)	(2)	(3)	(4)	(5)
	I Must Have That Man	18 Sep 1936	Par F575	(188)

THOMAS "FATS" WALLER
(b 21 May 1904; d 15 December 1943)

FATS WALLER AND HIS CONTINENTAL RHYTHM:
Fats Waller (piano, celeste & organ); Dave Wilkins (tpt); George Chisholm (tbn); Alfie Kahn (tenor sax & clar); Ian Sheppard (tenor sax & vln); Alan Ferguson (gtr); Len Harrison (bass); Harry Schneider (drs on first title only); Edmundo Ros (drs on remaining titles)

(1)	(2)	(3)	(4)	(5)
C149	Don't Try Your Jive On Me (Fats Waller)	21 Aug 1938	HMV BD5415	C150
	Ain't Misbehavin' (Fats Waller)	21 Aug 1938	HMV BD5415	C147 C150
	The Flat Foot Floogie (Fats Waller)	21 Aug 1938	HMV BD5399	C150
	Pent Up In A Penthouse (Fats Waller)	21 Aug 1938	HMV BD5399	C150

(1)	(2)	(3)	(4)	(5)
	Music, Maestro, Please (Fats Waller)	21 Aug 1938	HMV BD5398	C150
	A-Tisket, A-Tasket (Fats Waller & Band)	21 Aug 1938	HMV BD5398	C150
	FATS WALLER (Piano Solos) Accompanied by Max Lewin (Drums):			
	London Suite - Piccadilly (N/V)	13 Jun 1939	HMV B10059	C150
	Chelsea (N/V)	13 Jun 1939	HMV B10059	C150
	Soho (N/V)	13 Jun 1939	HMV B10060	C150
	Bond Street (N/V)	13 Jun 1939	HMV B10060	C150
	Limehouse (N/V)	13 Jun 1939	HMV B10061	C150
	Whitechapel (N/V)	13 Jun 1939	HMV B10061	C150

FRANK WEIR
(b 1911; d 12 May 1981)

	FRANK WEIR AND HIS ORCHESTRA:			
C174	All Through The Day (Vivien Paget)	21 Jul 1946	Dec Unissued take (F8659)	

JACK WHITE
(b 2 December 1905)

	JACK WHITE AND HIS ORCHESTRA:			
C174	I'll Dance At Your Wedding (N/V)	20 Apr 1948	Dec F8905	

MARK WHITE

	MARK WHITE Presents "JAZZ CLUB":			
	Freddy Randall (tpt); Geoff Love (tnb); Cliff Townshend (clar); Laurie Gold (tenor sax); Dill Jones (pno); Vic Lewis (gtr); Hank Hobson (bass); Max Abrams (drs)			
C142	Black And Blue (N/V)	24 Feb 1949	Dec F9136	(C44 C50 C120)
	Jack Jackson (tpt); Nobby Clark (tbm); Sid Phillips (clar); Mickey Lewis (alto sax); Harry Gold (tenor & bass saxes); Billy Munn (pno); Jack Llewellyn (gtr); Will Hemmings (bass); Max Abrams (drs)			
C143	Davenport Blues (N/V)	23 Feb 1949	Dec F9214	

JAY WILBUR
(d 12 March 1969)

	JAY WILBUR AND HIS BAND:			
C175	Five O'Clock Whistle (Dorothy Carless)	17 Jan 1941	Rex Unissued take (9915)	(C105 C120)
	We Three (My Echo, My Shadow And Me) (Dorothy Carless)	17 Jan 1941	Rex Unissued take (9915)	(C105)

MAURICE WINNICK
(b 1902; d 28 May 1962)

	MAURICE WINNICK AND HIS BAND:			
C174	I'm Keeping Company (Harry Bentley)	11 Sep 1931	EBW 5388	
	What More Can I Ask? (Jimmy Messini)	9 Jan 1933	Pan 25435	

ERIC WINSTONE
(b 1 January 1915; d 2 May 1974)

	ERIC WINSTONE AND HIS BAND:			
C167	Stage Coach (N/V)	10 Jan 1942	R[illegible] MR3595	(C38 C48)

SECTION 2

COLLECTIONS

Explanatory Notes

Albums listed in this section of the Supplement contain collections of tracks by different bands amd orchestras, and in some cases artists outside the scope of the Supplement. They bear a reference number prefixed with the letter 'C', and to maintain continuity, they are numbered in sequence from the number last used in the corresponding section of the Catalogue.

Basic details only of bands and tune titles shown in this section. Information relating to vocalists, recording dates and 78rpm labels etc will be found in Section 1 under the respective bandleader's name by referring either to the corresponding Collection reference number or, in instances where a recording has been duplicated in a Complete Album or another Collection, to the reference number shown after the tune title. For example, details of Harry Roy recording of "Bugle Call Rag" which is included in Collection C164, will be found in Section 1 under Harry Roy's name (Titles contained in Collections only) by referring to reference C164 in Column (1). Details of the Harry Roy recording of "Troublesome Trumpet" which is contained in Collection C164, but which shows a reference number of 224 after the tune title, will be found in Section 1 under Album 224 in which it is also included.

To conserve space and for ease of reference, it should be noted that tune titles in these Collections are not listed in album playing order but are grouped together under respective bandleaders' names in alphabetical order.

E.T.

C142 Scrapbook Of British Jazz : Decca LK4139*

GEORGE CHISHOLM & JIVE FIVE
Rosetta
FRED ELIZALDE & MUSIC
Clarinet Marmalade
NAT GONELLA (With Instr Accomp)
Georgia On My Mind
SPIKE HUGHES & DANCE ORCH
The Moochi
SID PHILLIPS' QUINTET
Royal Garden Blues
GEORGE SHEARING QUARTET
Afraid Of You
LEW STONE & BAND
White Jazz
MARK WHITE'S "JAZZ CLUB"
Black And Blue

Note: The remaining tracks in this album, which are outside the scope of the Supplement, are by Chris Barber's Jazz Band, Ken Colyer's Jazzmen, Harry Gold & His Pieces Of Eight ("Skeleton Jangle" recorded on 16 Oct 1950) and George Webb's Dixielanders.

C143 Scrapbook Of British Jazz - Volume 2 : Decca LK4205*

GEORGE CHISHOLM & JIVE FIVE
You'll Always Be Mine
GEORGE CHISHOLM & JIVE EIGHT
Broadhurst Garden Blues
FRED ELIZALDE & MUSIC
Stomp Your Feet
SPIKE HUGHES & ORCH
Doan' You Grieve
JACK HYLTON & ORCH
Some Of These Days
SID PHILLIPS' QUINTET
Strut Miss Lizzie
DANNY POLO & SWING STARS
Stratton Street Strut
MARK WHITE'S "JAZZ CLUB"
Davenport Blues

Note: The remaining tracks in this album, which are outside the scope of the Supplement, are by Ken Colyer's Jazzmen, Wally Fawkes-Sandy Brown Quintet, George Melly with Alex Welsh Dixielanders and George Webb's Dixielanders.

C144 The World Of George Formby : Decca PA/SPA 50*

JACK HYLTON & ORCH/George Formby
Why Don't Women Like Me?
The Old Kitchen Kettle
Chinese Laundry Blues
Running Round The Fountains In Trafalgar Square
Sitting On The Ice At The Ice Rink

Note: The remaining tracks in this album are by George Formby with other accompaniments.

C145 The World Of George Formby - Volume 2 : Decca SPA 446*

JACK HYLTON & ORCH/George Formby
Do De O Do
I Told My Baby With My Ukulele

Note: The remaining tracks in this album are by George Formby with other accompaniments.

C146 Remembering The 40's (8-Record Boxed Set) : Reader's Digest GREM-A-035*

AMBROSE & ORCH
Coming In On A Wing And A Prayer
BILLY COTTON & BAND
I'm Going To Get Lit-Up
Sailor, Who Are You Dreaming Of Tonight?
I've Got A Lovely Bunch Of Coconuts
BILLY MAYERL
Room Five-Hundred-And-Four
JACK PAYNE & BAND
It's A Lovely Day Tomorrow
EDMUNDO ROS & RUMBA BAND
Manana (Is Soon Enough For Me) 223
The Coffee Song 223
PRIMO SCALA'S ACCORDEON BAND (H.BIDGOOD)
Roll Me Over
PRIMO SCALA'S ACCORDEON BAND (H.BIDGOOD)
My Love Is Only For You
SQUADRONAIRES
Five Minutes More
Cement Mixer
The Wishing Waltz
LEW STONE & NOVA-TONES
Let It Snow, Let It Snow, Let It Snow

Note: The remaining tracks in this set are by British and American popular artists of the period, including the following: Hoagy Carmichael, Perry Como, Bing Crosby & the Andrews Sisters, Denny Dennis, Tommy Dorsey & Orch, Flanagan &

Allen, Reggie Goff, Dick Haymes, Eddie Heywood, Guy Lombardo & Royal Canadians, Vera Lynn, Glenn Miller & Orch and the Mills Brothers.

C147 Harlem Comes To London : World Records SH 265*

VALAIDA
I Can't Dance
I Must Have That Man
FATS WALLER & CONTINENTAL RHYTHM
Ain't Misbehavin' C149

Note: Remaining tracks are by Buck & Bubbles, Lavaida Carter, Duke Ellington & Orch, Adelaide Hall, Ike Hatch, Nicholas Brothers, Plantation Orchestra, Noble Sissle & Orch and Elizabeth Welch.

Produced by Chris Ellis
Transferred by John Wadley
Sleeve Note by Brian Rust

C148 The Fabulous Finn (Sylvester Ahola) : Quality QRS 1001 (USA)

AMBROSE & ORCH
A Girl Friend Of A Boy Friend Of Mine
ARCADIANS DANCE ORCH (B.FIRMAN)
Sunny Skies
When I Met Connie In The Cornfield
PHILIP LEWIS & ORCH
Tiger Rag
Button Up Your Overcoat
THE NIGHT CLUB KINGS (R.NOBLE)
Someone
In The Moonlight
THE PICCADILLY PLAYERS
Kiss And Make Up
THE RHYTHMIC EIGHT (B.FIRMAN)
I Ain't Got Nobody
Can't Help Lovin' Dat Man
THE RHYTHM MANIACS (P.LEWIS)
That's A-Plenty
RAY STARITA & AMBASSADORS CLUB BAND
Rhapsody In Rhythm

Note: The remaining track in this album is by the Georgians (USA) playing "Frisco Bay" (recorded on 14 January 1927.

C149 Fats Waller In London (2-Record Set) : World Records SHB 29*

FATS WALLER & CONTINENTAL RHYTHM
Don't Try Your Jive On Me
Ain't Misbehavin'
The Flat Foot Floogie
Pent Up In A Penthouse
Music, Maestro, Please
A-Tisket, A-Tasket
FATS WALLER (Piano)
London Suite - Piccadilly/Chelsea
Soho/Bond Street
Limehouse/Whitechapel

Note: The remainder of this set consists of piano solos by Fats Waller (recorded in New York in 1922); organ solos by Waller (recorded in London), and vocals by Adelaide Hall accompanied by Waller at the Compton organ.

C150 Fats Waller In London : EMI Retrospect Series EG 26 0442 1

FATS WALLER & CONTINENTAL RHYTHM
Don't Try Your Jive On Me C149
Ain't Misbehavin' C149
The Flat Foot Floogie C149
Pent Up In A Penthouse C149
Music, Maestro, Please C149
A-Tisket, A-Tasket C149
FATS WALLER (Piano)
London Suite - Piccadilly/Chelsea C149
Soho/Bond Street C149
Limehouse/Whitechapel C149

Note: Four remaining tracks in this album feature organ solos by Fats Waller and vocals by Adelaide Hall with accompaniment by Waller at the Compton organ.

Produced & Compiled by Chris Ellis
Transferred & Remastered by John Wadley
Sleeve Note by Brian Rust

C151 Rhythm Is Our Business - Django Reinhardt and Stephane Grappelli : Decca TAB 55

STEPHANE GRAPPELLY & MUSICANS
Noel Brings The Swing
I Never Knew
Sweet Sue, Just You
STEPHANE GRAPPELLY & QUARTET
Jive Bomber
Dinah
STEPHANE GRAPPELLY & QUINTET
Au Revoir
Stardust

Note: The remainder of this album consists of 4 tracks by the Quintet Of The Hot Club Of France, recorded in 1939; and 5 tracks by Stephane Grappelly and His Hot Four (of French origin), recorded in 1935.

Compiled by Alun Morgan
Transferred by Colin Brown
Sleeve Note by Vic Bellerby

C152 Running Wild - The Original Sounds Of The Jazz Age (1921-1931) : Living Era AJA 5017

JACK HYLTON & ORCH
Painting The Clouds With Sunshine

Remaining tracks are by Gene Austin Rube Bloom & Bayou Boys, Boswell Sisters, California Ramblers, Maurice Chevalier, Frank Crumit, Cliff Edwards, Duke Ellington & Orch, Ruth Etting, Annette Hanshaw, Al Jolson, Ted Lewis & Band, Nick Lucas, McKinney's Cotton Pickers, Original Dixieland Jazz Band, Jimmie Rodgers, Sophie Tucker, Rudy Vallee & Connecticut Yankees, Fats Waller, Ted Weems & Orch and Paul Whiteman & Orch

Produced by Kevin Daly
Sleeve Note by Brian Rust

C153 Al Bowlly - Twenty Golden Greats : EMI SCA 060 (Australian)

NEW MAYFAIR DANCE ORCH (R.NOBLE)
Time On My Hands
Goodnight Sweetheart 220
RAY NOBLE & NEW MAYFAIR DANCE ORCH
Love Is The Sweetest Thing 220
Looking On The Bright Side Of Life
RAY NOBLE & ORCH
The Very Thought Of You 220
Please
A Little Street Where Old Friends Meet
Have You Ever Been Lonely?
The Moment I Saw You
The Old Spinning Wheel
Thanks
My Song Goes Round The World
Did You Ever See A Dream Walking?
I Love You Truly
All I Do Is Dream Of You 221
NOVELTY ORCH (R.NOBLE)
You're Driving Me Crazy
SAVOY HOTEL ORPHEANS (C.GIBBONS)
Sweet And Lovely

Note: Threee remaining tracks in this album feature Al Bowlly in a solo capacity. The titles are:
Dark Eyes (rec 11 May 1939)
Over The Rainbow (rec 21 Dec 1939)
It's A Lovely Day Tomorrow (rec 15 Feb 1940)

C154 Comic Cuts - Classic Comedy Items (1926-1934) : Old Bean Records OLD 2

AMBROSE & ORCH
The Sun Has Got His Hat On
BBC DANCE ORCH (H.HALL)
Who's Afraid Of The Big Bad Wolf?
JACK HYLTON & ORCH/George Formby
Chinese Laundry Blues
JACK HYLTON & ORCH
Is Izzy Azzy Wozz?
NEW MAYFAIR DANCE ORCH (R.NOBLE)
Blaze Away
RAY NOBLE & ORCH
All Over Italy
Wheezy Anna
JACK PAYNE & BBC DANCE ORCH
I Faw Down And Go Boom 222
Airman! Airman!
Sing Holly, Go Whistle, Hey! Hey!
JACK PAYNE AND BAND
Let's All Sing Like The Birdies Sing
DEBROY SOMERS' BAND
I'm Going Back To Himazaz

Note: Remaining tracks are by Gracie Fields (2), Leslie Holmes, Stanley Lupino, Charles Penrose and Leslie Sarony.

C155 A Cole Porter Collection : Stash ST 127 (Canadian)

CARROLL GIBBONS & SAVOY HOTEL ORPHEANS
Rosalie
JACK PAYNE & BBC DANCE ORCH
Love For Sale

Remaining tracks are by Banjo Buddy, Don Bestor & Orch, Emil Coleman & Orch, Tommy Dorsey & Orch, Mary Healey, Richard Himber & Ritz-Carlton Hotel Orch, Frances Langford, Vincent Lopez & Orch, Ray Noble & Orch (USA), Artie Shaw & New Music, Martha Tilton, Bea Wain, Ethel Waters and Paul Whiteman & Orch.

C156 The Great British Dance Bands Play The Music Of Cole Porter : EMI Retrospect Series EG 26 0443 1

BBC DANCE ORCH (H.HALL)
Anything Goes
Easy To Love
I've Got You Under My Skin
GERALDO & ORCH
Begin The Beguine
Don't Fence Me In
GERALDO & SAVOY HOTEL ORCH
Ridin' High
CARROLL GIBBONS & SAVOY HOTEL ORPHEANS
It's D'Lovely
I've Got My Eyes On You
Do I Love You, Do I?
You'd Be So Nice To Come Home To
JACK HYLTON & ORCH
Let's Do It
What Is This Thing Called Love?
Love For Sale
You're The Top
My Heart Belongs To Daddy
RAY NOBLE & ORCH
Experiment
HARRY ROY & ORCH
Night And Day
Miss Otis Regrets
I Get A Kick Out Of You
HARRY ROY & BAND
Let's Be Buddies

Note: This album is a compilation of tracks from Album (C10)

Produced & Transferred by Chris Ellis
Sleeve Note by Brian Rust

C157 The Song Is....Jerome Kern : Living Era AJA 5036

AMBROSE & ORCH
She Didn't Say 'Yes'
They Didn't Believe Me
BBC DANCE ORCH (H.HALL)
The Song Is You
LEW STONE & BAND
Hand In Hand

Remaining tracks are by Emil Coleman & Riviera Orch (2), Mary Ellis, Claude Hopkins & Orch, Ipana Troubadors, Marilyn Miller & Lawrence Gray, Helen Morgan (2), Paul Robeson and Paul Whiteman & Orch (3).

Produced by Kevin & Tony Baldwin
Sleeve Note by Brian Rust

C158 The Song Is....Richard Rodgers And Lorenz Hart : Living Era AJA 5041

JACK HYLTON & ORCH
Maybe It's Me
SAVOY ORPHEANS
The Blue Room

Remaining tracks are by Victor Arden & Phil Ohman & Their Orch, George Baker & Derek Oldham, Bix Beiderbecke & Gang, Sam Coslow, Bing Crosby, Hutch (Leslie A.Hutchinson), Jessie Matthews, Leo Reisman & Orch, Stuart Ross & Joe Sargent, Frankie Trumbauer & Orch and Roger Wolfe Kahn & Orch.

Produced by Kevin Daly & Tony Baldwin
Sleeve Note by Brian Rust

C159 Elsie Carlisle - She's The Talk Of The Town : Conifer CHD 126

AMBROSE & ORCH
No! No! A Thousand Times No
Home James, And Don't Spare The Horses
I'm Gonna Wash My Hands Of You

Note: The remaining tracks in this album feature Elsie Carlisle in a solo capacity, and were recorded between 1932 and 1934.

Produced & Transferred by Colin Brown
Sleeve Note by Frank Stapleton

C160 Billy Amstell - Don't Fuss Mr. Ambrose (2-Record Set) : Decca Recollections RFLD 51

AMBROSE & ORCH
Nevertheless
My Romance
La Di Da Di Da
The Very Thought Of You
La Cucaracha
Okay Toots
Streamline Strut
B'Wanga
Life Begins When You're In Love
Hide And Seek
Organ Grinder's Swing
Tarantula
Power House
Swing Is In The Air
Mr. Reynard's Nightmare
Voo Doo
Tootin' Around
Beer Barrel Polka
The Penguin
War Dance Of The Wooden Indians
If A Grey-Haired Lady Says 'How's Yer Father?'
STANLEY BLACK & MODERNISTS
Swanee
I Ain't Got Nobody
BLUE MOUNTAINEERS
When We're Alone
Sweet Sixteen And Never Been Kissed
LOUIS DE VRIES & RHYTHM BOYS
St. Louis Blues
Moonglow
EMBASSY RHYTHM EIGHT
Hitchy Koo
He's A Rag Picker
ROY FOX & BAND
A Peach Of A Pair
I'm So Used To You Now
Leave The Rest to Nature
JACK HARRIS & ORCH
You Brought A New Kind Of Love To Me
The Moon Is Low

Note: Two remaining tracks in this set are of solo recordings by Elsie Carlisle ("Without That Certain Thing") and Doris Hare ("The Old Man Of The Mountain").

Compiled & Remastered by Colin Brown
Sleeve Note by Tony Clarke

C161 These Foolish Things 1936 : Phontastic NOST 7658 (Swedish)

BILLY COTTON & BAND
Shoe Shine Boy

Remaining tracks are by Fred Astaire, Bunny Berigan & Orch, Bing Crosby with Louis Armstrong & Frances Langford, Bob Crosby & Orch, Tommy Dorsey & Orch, Duke Ellington & Orch, Benny Goodman & Orch, Jimmie Lunceford & Orch, Ben Pollock & Orch, Fats Waller & Rhythm and Teddy Wilson & Orch.

Produced by Anders R. Ohman
Transferred by Gert Palmerantz
Sleeve Note by Anders R. Ohman

C162 Spike Hughes & His Dance Orchestra & His Three Blind Mice 1930 - Volume 2 : Retrieval FG 409

PHILIP BUCHEL With SPIKE HUGHES & THREE BLIND MICE
You Know What I'll Do
Happy Feet
JIMMY DORSEY Accomp BY SPIKE HUGHES & THREE BLIND MICE
I'm Just Wild About Harry
After You've Gone
Tiger Rag (Take-1)
Tiger Rag (Take-2)
St. Louis Blues
SPIKE HUGHES & DANCE ORCH
Poor Butterfly
SPIKE HUGHES & DANCE ORCH
Kalua
Dancing Time
I Like To Do Things For You
Happy Feet
Harlem Madness
Blue Turning Grey Over You
Margie
Cinderella Browne

Produced, Transferred & Remastered by John R.T. Davies
Sleeve Note by Leslie Thompson

C163 The Best Of British Dance Bands - Extracts From The Saville Records Catalogue : Saville SVL 177

AMBROSE & ORCH
Happy Days Are Here Again
I'm In The Market For You
BBC DANCE ORCH (H.HALL)
How Can You Say 'No'?
BILLY COTTON & BAND
It's The Girl
Too Many Tears
FRED ELIZALDE'S RHYTHMICIANS
After The Sun Kissed The World Goodbye
ROY FOX & BAND
By The River Sainte Marie
The Wind's In The West
CARROLL GIBBONS & SAVOY HOTEL ORPHEANS
My Silent Love
For All We Know 205
JACK HYLTON & ORCH
Honeymoon Hotel
JACK JACKSON & ORCH
Play To Me Gypsy 213
Kiss Me Dear
NEW MAYFAIR DANCE ORCH (C.GIBBONS)
Good Little, Bad Little You
NEW MAYFAIR DANCE ORCH (RAY NOBLE)
Any Time's The Time To Fall In Love
JACK PAYNE & BBC DANCE ORCH
My Baby Just Cares For Me 222
HARRY ROY & ORCH
Like Taking Candy From A Baby
Say It
SAVOY ORPHEANS
Baby Face
RAY STARITA & AMBASSADORS CLUB BAND
Crazy Rhythm

Produced & Transferred by John Wadley

C164 Harry Roy And His Orchestra - Hotcha-Ma-Cha-Cha : Living Era AJA 5035

HARRY ROY & ORCH
Troublesome Trumpet 224
Eadie Was A Lady
Bugle Call Rag
Mama Don't Want No Peas And Rice And Coconut Oil
Lover*
Build A Little Home
Black Panther
Rock And Roll
There's A New Day Comin'
Twelfth Street Rag
When A St. Louis Woman Comes Down To New Orleans
Canadian Capers
The Roy Rag
Let's Call It A Day*
SYD ROY'S LYRICALS
Stay Out Of The South
My Pet

*Original issues as Leslie Hutchinson accompanied by Harry Roy and His Orchestra.

Produced by Kevin Daly & Tony Baldwin
Sleeve Note by Brian Rust

C165 Monte Rey - Song Of Songs : Conifer CHD 130

GERALDO & GAUCHO TANGO ORCH
Yira, Yira
Vida Mia
Donde
GERALDO & ORCH
Without A Song
Beyond The Blue Horizon
I Surrender, Dear
In My Little Red Book
Balloons

Note: Ten more tracks in this album feature Monte Rey in a solo capacity. The accompaniments on these are provided by Sidney Torch (Organ); Orchestra directed by Philip Green; and unknown piano and violin.

Produced & Transferred by Colin Brown
Sleeve Note by Hugh Palmer

C166 The Golden Age Of Larry Adler : EMI GX 41 2539 1

CARROLL GIBBONS & SAVOY HOTEL ORPHEANS Accompanying Larry Adler (Harmonica)
Rhapsody In Blue, Parts 1 & 2
RONNIE MUNRO & ORCH Accompanying Larry Adler (Harmonica)
I've Got You Under My Skin
They All Laughed
I've Got My Love To Keep Me Warm/Slumming On Park Avenue
Caravan
Night And Day/Tiger Rag

GEORGE SCOTT WOOD & ORCH Accompanying Larry Adler (Harmonica)
Stormy Weather

Note: The remaining tracks in this feature Larry Adler with other accompaniments, some including the Quintet Of The Hot Club Of France.

Produced & Compiled by Hugh Palmer
Transferred by Peter Bown
Sleeve Note by Larry Adler

C167 Down Memory Lane - A Salute To The 40's (8-Record Boxed Set) : Reader's Digest GDML-A-152

BILLY COTTON & BAND
I've Got Sixpence
Ma, I Miss Your Apple Pie
This Is The Army, Mr. Jones
GERALDO & ORCH
I Couldn't Sleep A Wink Last Night
CARROLL GIBBONS & SAVOY HOTEL ORPHEANS
Mary Lou
NAT GONELLA & GEORGIANS
One Meat Ball
ROBERTO INGLEZ & ORCH
The Green Cockatoo
JOE LOSS & ORCH
Let Him Go, Let Him Tarry
FELIX MENDELSSOHN & HAWAIIAN SERENADERS
Paradise Isle
HARRY ROY & BAND
Leicester Square Rag
ERIC WINSTONE & BAND
Stage Coach

Note: The remaining tracks in this set are by British and American popular artists of the period, including the following: Andrews Sisters, Issy Bonn, Sam Browne, Dorothy Carless, Steve Conway, Noel Coward, Bing Crosby, Jimmy Dorsey & Orch, Gracie Fields, Flanagan & Allen, Judy Garland, Ink Spots, Kay Kyser & Orch, Evelyn Laye, Turner Layton, Archie Lewis, Celia Lipton, Vera Lynn, Glenn Miller & Orch, Vaughan Munroe & Orch, Anne Shelton, Dinah Shore, Dorothy Squires, Richard Tauber, Tommy Trinder and Dooley Wilson.

C168 Thanks For The Memories (1940's & 1950's) (8-Record Boxed Set) : Reader's Digest GTHA-A-125

TED HEATH & MUSIC
Sabre Dance
Mountain Greenery
SQUADRONAIRES
You're Driving Me Crazy

Note: The remaining tracks in this set are by British and American popular artists of the period, including the following: Leroy Anderson & Orch Andrews Sisters, Louis Armstrong & All Stars, Beverley Sisters, Les Brown & Band, Frank Chacksfield & Orch, Rosemary Clooney, Perry Como, Bing Crosby, Eric Delaney & Orch, Duke Ellington & Orch, Four Aces, Judy Garland, Jascha Heifetz, Ink Spots, Anton Karas, Danny Kaye, Peggy Lee, Vera Lynn, Mantovani & Orch, Mary Martin, Glenn Miller & Orch, Mills Brothers, Carmen Miranda, Joan Regan, Lita Roza, Anne Shelton, Cyril Stapleton & Orch and Dickie Valentine.

C169 British Dance Bands Of The 40's (2-Record Set) : London Recollections RECDL 2

AMBROSE & ORCH
If I Had My Way
More And More
The Cookhouse Serenade
Better Not Roll Those Blue Blue Eyes
An Hour Never Passes
I Threw A Kiss In The Ocean
The Shrine Of Saint Cecilia
My Wubba Dolly
Coming In On A Wing And A Prayer C146
LEW STONE & BAND
It's A Blue World
In A Little Rocky Valley
There's Nothing New To Tell You
Sing A Round-Up Song
Too Romantic
The Hut-Sut Song
A Mother's Prayer At Twilight
And So Do I
We'll Meet Again
ROYAL AIR FORCE DANCE ORCH
Keep An Eye On Your Heart
Blue Champagne
It's Foolish But It's Fun
Out Of Nowhere
There I Go
The Whistler's Mother-In-Law
Lover's Lullaby
All Our Tomorrows
You Started Something

OSCAR RABIN & BAND
An Apple For The Teacher
You're Mine
When Night Is Thru'
Sometimes
A Man And His Dream
Moonlight Avenue
When The Rose Of Tralee Met Danny Boy
Basin Street Ball
Sing, Everybody, Sing

Compiled & Remastered by Colin Brown
Sleeve Note by John Tracy

C170 George Formby - Leaning On A Lamp Post (2-Record Set) : London Recollections RECDL 4

JACK HYLTON & ORCH/George Formby
Do De O Do C145
Chinese Laundry Blues C144
I Told My Baby with My Ukulele C145
If You Don't Want The Goods, Don't Maul 'Em
The Old Kitchen Kettle C144
Why Don't Women Like Me? C144
Running Round The Fountains In Trafalgar Square C144
Sitting On The Ice At The Ice Rink C144
Levi's Monkey Mike

Note: The remaining tracks in this set are by George Formby with other accompaniments.

Compiled by Colin Brown & John Tracy
Remastered by Colin Brown
Sleeve Note by John Tracy

C171 Songs Of Christmas Past : London Recollections RECOL 7

PRIMO SCALA'S BANJO & ACCORDEON BAND
Jingle Bells (H.BIDGOOD)

Note: The rest of this album consists of tracks of Christmas inspired songs (most of which were recorded in the 1950 s) by the following artists: Beverley Sisters, Billy Cotton & Band, Four Ramblers, Dave King, Archie Lewis, Vera Lynn, Lita Roza, Primo Scala, Anne Shelton, Dickie Valentine and David Whitfield.

Compiled & Remastered by Colin Brown
Sleeve Note by John Tracy

C172 They Played The Hippodrome (2-Record Set) : London Recollections RECDL 11

AMBROSE & ORCH
Breathless
JOHNNY DENIS & NOVELTY SWINGTET
Dream
NAT GONELLA & GEORGIANS
Murder
HATCHETT'S SWINGTETTE
Papa's In Bed With His Breeches On
CHARLIE KUNZ (Piano with rhythm accomp)
Piano Medley No. D84
PRIMO SCALA'S BANJO & ACCORDEON BAND
Underneath The Arches (HLBODGOOD)
SQUADRONAIRES/Sam Browne
Reflections On The Water
BILLY TERNENT & ORCH
I Like Riding On A Choo Choo

Note: The remaining tracks in this set, some of which were recorded in the 1950s, are by Larry Adler, Issy Bonn, Charlie Chester, Beryl Davis ("My Heart Isn't In It", recorded 20 Jul 1946), Flanagan & Allen, Cyril Fletcher, George Formby, Adelaide Hall, Tommy Handley, Dick James ("In All The World", recorded 13 Oct 1949), Lupino Lane, Archie Lewis, Norman Long, Cavan O'Connor, Tessie O'Shea, Sandy Powell, Ralph Reader, Lita Roza, Anne Shelton ("Put Your Shoes On Lucy", recorded 3 Feb 1949), Frankie Vaughan, Nellie Wallace, Elsie & Doris Waters, Jimmy Wheeler, Bertha Willmott and Eric Whitley.

Compiled & Remastered by Colin Brown
Sleeve Note by John Tracy

C173 Stephane Grappelly - I Got Rhythm (2-Record Set) : London Recollections RECDL 12

STEPHANE GRAPPELLEY & MUSICANS
After You've Gone
Stephane's Tune
Tiger Rag
Stephane's Blues
Sweet Sue, Just You C151
Noel Brings The Swing C151
STEPHANE GRAPPELLY & QUARTET
Dinah C151
Jive Bomber C151

STEPHANE GRAPPELLY & QUARTET
Heavenly Music
Star Eyes
My Heart Tells Me
I Never Mention Your Name
I'm Confessin' (That I Love You)
Someday Sweetheart
Don't You Know I Care?
No One Else Will Do
STEPHANE GRAPPELLY & QUINTET
Liza (All The Clouds'll Roll Away)
The Folks Who Live On The Hill
When I Look At You
Weep No More, My Lady
Three O'Clock In The Morning
That Old Black Magic
HATCHETT'S SWINGTETTE
You Made Me Love You

HATCHETT'S SWINGTETTE
Alexander's Ragtime Band
Ting-A-Ling (The Waltz Of The Bells)
Scatterbrain
It's A Hap-Hap-Happy Day
Bluebirds In The Moonlight
Oh Johnny, Oh Johnny, Oh!
Lady Be Good
In The Mood
I Got Rhythm
Playmates
Oh! By Jingo, Oh! By Gee
The Sheik Of Araby
I Said "No"

Compiled & Remastered by Colin Brown
Sleeve Note by John Tracy

C174 Dancing The Night Away (2-Record Set) : London Recollections RECDL 16

AMBROSE & ORCH
Rehearsing A Lullaby
THE BARNSTORMERS
La Di Da Di Da
AL COLLINS & ORCH
Moon Over Miami
MIFF FERRIE & FERRYMEN
Sweetheart Of All My Dreams
ROY FOX & BAND
Ya Got Love
You're Telling Me
GERALDO & ORCH
Will You Remember (Sweetheart)?
NAT GONELLA & GEORGIANS
Gnat Jump
One Meat Ball C167
HENRY HALL & GLENEAGLES HOTEL BAND
I Was True
JACK HARRIS & ORCH
On The Sunny Side Of The Street
HATCHETT'S SWINGTETTE
Beat Me Daddy, Eight To A Bar
JACK JACKSON & ORCH
The New Swing Alphabet
KEN JOHNSON & WEST INDIAN DANCE ORCH
Snakehips Swing
TEDDY JOYCE & DANCE MUSIC
I Never Had A Change
FELIX KING, HIS PIANO & ORCH
What Do I Have To Do (To Make You Love Me?)
TOMMY KINSMAN & DANCE BAND
Stardust
CHARLIE KUNZ & CASANI CLUB ORCH
Crying My Heart Out For You
SYDNEY KYTE & PICCADILLY HOTEL BAND
Lazybones
BRIAN LAWRENCE & LANSDOWNE ORCH
You're Looking For Romance, I'm Looking For Love
SYDNEY LIPTON & GROSVENOR HOUSE ORCH
Supposin'

JOE LOSS & BAND
In A Little Rocky Valley
BRAM MARTIN & BAND
The Waves Of The Ocean Are Whisp'ring Goodnight
BILLY MERRIN & COMMANDERS
There's A Ring Around The Moon
ROLAND PEACHEY & ROYAL HAWAIIANS
I Got Rhythm
SID PHILLIPS' QUINTET
Ridin' High
OSCAR RABIN & BAND
My Wubba Dolly
OSCAR RABIN & STRICT TEMPO DANCE BAND
Dancing Time
EDMUNDO ROS & RUMBA BAND
Quien No Llora No Mama
HARRY ROY & ORCH
Sambina
The Darktown Strutters' Ball
RAY STARITA & AMBASSADORS BAND
The Old Man Of The Mountain
LEW STONE & MONSEIGNEUR BAND
My Heart's To Let
LEW STONE & STONECRACKERS
Get Happy
LEW STONE & NOVA-TONES
I'll Buy That Dream
NAT TEMPLE & CLUB ROYAL ORCH
Nattering Around
FRANK WEIR & ORCH
All Through The Day
JACK WHITE & ORCH
I'll Dance At Your Wedding
MAURICE WINNICK & BAND
I'm Keeping Company
What More Can I Ask?

Compiled & Remastered by Colin Brown
Sleeve Note by John Tracy

C175 Whispering Grass - Dorothy Carless/Benny Lee/Adelaide Hall/Issy Bonn (2-Record Set) : London Recollections RECDL 19

HATCHETT'S SWINGTETTE
Beat Me Daddy, Eight To A Bar C174
LEW STONE & BAND
I Hear A Rhapsody
Number Ten Lullaby Lane
When They Sound The Last "All Clear"
As If You Didn't Know
Why Don't We Do This More Often?
I Guess I'll Have To Dream The Rest
Lonely Serenade
We Both Told A Lie
What More Can I Say?
JAY WILBUR & BAND
Five O'Clock Whistle
We Three (My Echo, My Shadow And Me)

Note: The rest of this set consists of 9 tracks by Adelaide Hall recorded between 27 Dec 1939 and 4 Aug 1944; 9 tracks by Issy Bonn recorded between 26 Oct 1943 and 24 Sep 1948; and the following tracks by Dorothy Carless:
How About You? (3 Apr 1942)
I'll Always Remember (3 Apr 1942)
Whispering Grass (7 Jul 1942)
Autumn Nocturne (7 Jul 1942)
(all with accompaniments by Eugene Pini & His Orchestra)
Jim (13 Feb 1942)
Do You Care? (13 Feb 1942)
(with accompaniments by Jay Wilbur & His Orchestra)

Compiled & Remastered by Colin Brown
Sleeve Note by John Tracy

C176 Music From The BBC-TV Serial "The Singing Detective" : BBC Records REN 608

AMBROSE & ORCH
Limehouse Blues
BBC DANCE ORCH (H.HALL)
The Teddy Bears' Picnic
RAY NOBLE & ORCH
The Very Thought Of You 220
JACK PAYNE & BAND
It's A Lovely Day Tomorrow C146
LOU PREAGER & ORCH
Cruising Down The River
LEW STONE & BAND
I Get Along Without You Very Well

Note: The remaining tracks in this album are by Lale Anderson, Bing Crosby & the Andrews Sisters, Duke Ellington & Orch, Ella Fitzgerald, Max Harris, Dick Haymes, The Ink Spots, Al Jolson, Vera Lynn, Mills Brothers, Anne Shelton and Fred Waring & Pennsylvanians.

Remastered by Paul Gillham & Bruce Talbot
Sleeve Note by Kenith Trodd

C177 Tiger Rag 1931 : Phontastic NOST 7619 (Swedish)

NEW MAYFAIR DANCE ORCH (RAY NOBLE)
Goodnight Sweetheart 220

Remaining tracks are by Louis Armstrong & Orch, Mildred Bailey with Paul Whiteman & Orch, Bing Crosby, Duke Ellington & Orch, Benny Goodman & Orch, Fletcher Henderson & Orch, Ted Lewis & Orch, Mills Brothers, Don Redman & Orch, Joe Venuti-Eddie Lang All Star Orch and Fats Waller.

Produced by Anders R. Ohman
Transferred by Gert Palmerantz
Sleeve Note by Anders R. Ohman

C178 The Wibbly Wobbly Walk - Novelty Numbers From Phonograph Cylinders & 78's : Saydisc SDL 350

THE KIT-CAT BAND
There's A Rickety Rackety Shack
SAVOY HAVANA BAND
Why Did I Kiss That Girl?

Note: Remaining tracks are by Jack Charman, Billy Merson, Billy Murray, Arthur Osmond, Premier Quartet, Tennessee Happy Boys, Walter Van Brunt, Billy Williams (all taken from Cylinders) and the Broadway Dance Orch (USA?), Columbia Novelty Orch, George Formby, Art Hickman & Orch (USA), International Novelty Quartet and Leslie Sarony (all taken from 78's).

C179 The song Is....Cole Porter : Living Era AJA 5044

AMBROSE & ORCH
All Through The Night
JACK HYLTON & ORCH
They All Fall In Love
LEW STONE & BAND
How Could We Be Wrong?

Note: Remaining tracks are by Anything Goes Foursome, Fred Astaire, Ben Bernie & Hotel Roosevelt Orch, Douglas Byng, Bing Crosby, Richard Himber & Ritz-Carlton Hotel Orch, Libby Holman, Gertrude Lawrence ("Experiment" with Ray Noble & Orch, rec 18 Oct 1933), Ethel Merman, Cole Porter and Leo Reisman & Orch.

Produced by Kevin Daly & Tony Baldwin
Sleeve Note by Geoff Milne

C180 The Golden Age Of The Male Vocal : EMI GX 41 2552 1

AMBROSE & ORCH
Dancing In The Dark 195
BBC DANCE ORCH (H. HALL)
The Music Goes Round And Around
ROY FOX & ORCH
Let's Face The Music And Dance 201
CARROLL GIBBONS & SAVOY HOTEL ORPHEANS
Sixty Seconds Got Together 206
JACK HYLTON & ORCH
Don't Let That Moon Get Away
JOE LOSS & BAND
Change Partners 217
RONNIE MUNRO & ORCH
Me And My Girl

Note: The remainder of the album contains tracks by Arthur Askey, Fred Astaire, Al Bowlly ("My Melancholy Baby" with Monia Liter, piano-taken from film soundtrack), Jack Buchanan, Maurice Chevalier, Noel Coward, Bobby Howes, Jack Hulbert and Hutch (Leslie A. Hutchinson).

C181 The Golden Age Of The Female Vocal : EMI GX 41 2553 1

AMBROSE & ORCH
Pu-Leeze! Mister Hemingway 195
GERALDO & SAVOY HOTEL ORCH
There Goes That Song Again 202
You've Done Something To My Heart
CARROLL GIBBONS & SAVOY HOTEL ORPHEANS
The Moon Got In My Eyes
LOUIS LEVY & ORCH
Says My Heart

Note: The ramainder of the album contains tracks by Cicely Courtneidge, Mary Ellis, Gracie Fields, Binnie Hale, Adelaide Hall (with Fats Waller, Organ), Frances Langford, Evelyn Laye, Jessie Matthews, Elizabeth Welch, Frances Williams and Peggy Wood.

SECTION 3

INDEX OF TUNE TITLES

The following Index lists Tune Titles included in the Supplement in alphabetical order. It shows the name of the band or orchestra that recorded the tune, together with the reference number(s) of the album(s) in which the recording is contained.

Where a recording by a particular band has also been included in an album contained in the original Catalogue, the reference number of the album conerned is shown in parenthesis; other numbers refer to albums included in the Supplement only. An asterisk (*) after a tune title denotes that other recordings of the tune are contained in the Catalogue.

In cases of tunes with an identical title, the names of the composers are shown in parenthesis as a means of identification.

Where a title forms part of a medley, or a show or film selection, the name of the medley or selection is shown in parenthesis after the tune title.

All My Life	SAVOY HOTEL ORPHEANS	205
All Our Tomorrows	ROYAL AIR FORCE DANCE ORCH	C169
All Over Italy	RAY NOBLE & ORCH	(125) C154
All Over The Place	ORGAN, THE DANCE BAND & ME	231
All Through The Day*	FRANK WEIR & ORCH	C174
All Through The Night*	AMBROSE & ORCH	C179
Alone* (Harry Roy Stage Show)	HARRY ROY & ORCH	225
A Lonely Singing Fool	JACK JACKSON & ORCH	(96) 213
A Man And His Dream	OSCAR RABIN & BAND	C169
Amapola*	JOE LOSS & ORCH	(107 C37) 219
Am I Blue?*	AMBROSE & ORCH	194
A Mother's Prayer At Twilight	LEW STONE & BAND	C169
An Apple For The Teacher*	OSCAR RABIN & BAND	C169
And So Do I	LEW STONE & BAND	C169
And The Angels Sing*	JOE LOSS & BAND	218
An Hour Never Passes	AMBROSE & ORCH	C169
A Nice Cup Of Tea	JOE LOSS & BAND	218
A Nightingale Sang In Berkeley Square*	C.GIBBONS & SAVOY HOTEL ORPHS	(56 C130) 206
An Old Italian Love Song*	AMBROSE & ORCH	194
Anything Goes*	BBC DANCE ORCH (HENRY HALL)	(C10) C156
(Cole Porter Suite)	LOUIS LEVY & MUSIC FROM MOVIES	215
Any Time's The Time To Fall In Love	NEW MAYFAIR DANCE OR (R.NOBLE)	(C121) C163
A Peach Of A Pair	ROY FOX & BAND	C160
Are You Havin' Any Fun?	JOE LOSS & BAND	(105 106) 217
Arkansas Traveller	GERALDO & ORCH	204
As If You Didn't Know	LEW STONE & BAND	C175
As Long As I Live	LEW STONE & BAND	(181) 229
A Street In Old Seville	BILLY COTTON & BAND	199
A-Tisket, A-Tasket*	FATS WALLER & CONTINENTAL RHYTHM	C149 C150
At The Balalaika*	JACK HYLTON & ORCH	212
At The Woodchoppers' Ball*	JOE LOSS & BAND	(105 107) 217
Au Revoir	STEPHANE GRAPPELLY & QUINTET	C151
Autumn Concerto	GERALDO & CONCERT ORCH	204
Babette		
(Carroll Re-Calls The Tunes No.1)	CARROLL GIBBONS (Piano solo)	207
Baby Face	SAVOY ORPHEANS	(C56 C137) C163
Back Beats*	SAVOY ORPHEANS	226
Balloons*	GERALDO & ORCH	C165
Basin Street Ball	OSCAR RABIN & BAND	C169
Beat Me Daddy, Eight To A Bar*	HATCHETT'S SWINGTETTE	(70 C107) C174 C175
Because It's Love*	AMBROSE & ORCH	196
	JACK JACKSON & ORCH	213
Beer Barrel Polka*	AMBROSE & ORCH	(15) C160
	JACK HYLTON & ORCH	212
Begin The Beguine*	GERALDO & ORCH	(C10) C156
	GERALDO & CONCERT ORCH	204
(Cole Porter Suite)	LOUIS LEVY & MUSIC FROM MOVIES	215
	VICTOR SILVESTER & BALLROOM ORCH	227
Beginner's Luck*	ROY FOX & ORCH	(41) 201
Best Wishes	BILLY COTTON & BAND	198
Better Not Roll Those Blue Blue Eyes	AMBROSE & ORCH	C169
Beyond The Blue Horizon	GERALDO & ORCH	C165
Bidin' My Time* (George Gershwin Suite)	LOUIS LEVY & MUSIC FROM THE MOVIES	215
Big Brass Band From Brazil	EDMUNDO ROS & RUMBA BAND	223
Black And Blue	MARK WHITE'S JAZZ CLUB	(C44 C50 C120) C142
Black Coffee*	NAT GONELLA & GEORGIANS	208
Black-Eyed Susan Brown*	MADAME TUSSAUD'S DANCE ORCH	197
Black Panther	HARRY ROY & ORCH	C164
Blaze Away	NEW MAYFAIR DANCE ORCH (R.NOBLE)	C154
Blondy*	JACK PAYNE & BBC DANCE ORCH	222
Blow, Gabriel, Blow	NAT GONELLA & GEORGIANS	(C10) 208
Blue Again	AMBROSE & ORCH	(7) 195

Bluebirds In The Moonlight*	HATCHETT'S SWINGTETTE	C173
Blue Champagne	ROYAL AIR FORCE DANCE ORCH	C169
Blue Evening Blues	SAVOY ORPHEANS	(C56) 226
Blue Lou*	VICTOR SILVESTER'S JIVE BAND	228
Blue Turning Grey Over You*	NAT GONELLA & GEORGIANS	209 210
	SPIKE HUGHES & DANCE ORCH	C162
Bond Street (From "London Suite")*	FATS WALLER (Piano solo)	C149 C150
Boo-Hoo*	JACK HYLTON & ORCH	212
	JOE LOSS & BAND	(105) 217
Boomps-A-Daisy	JOE LOSS & BAND	(105) 217
Boom! (Why Does My Heart Go Boom?)*	JOE LOSS & BAND	218
Boston Bounce*	VICTOR SILVESTER'S JIVE BAND	(C41) 228
Breathless	AMBROSE & ORCH	C172
Brighter Than The Sun*	SAVOY HOTEL ORPHEANS	205
Broadhurst Garden blues	GEORGE CHISHOLM & JIVE EIGHT	C143
Bubbling Over	CARROLL GIBBONS (Piano solo)	207
Bugle Call Rag*	BILLY COTTON & BAND	198
	HARRY ROY & ORCH	(156 159) C164
Build A Little Home*	HARRY ROY & ORCH	(157 C17) C164
But Not For Me (George Gershwin Suite)	LOUIS LEVY & MUSIC FROM MOVIES	215
Button Up Your Overcoat*	PHILIP LEWIS & ORCH	C148
B'Wanga	AMBROSE & ORCH	(11) C160
By A Waterfall*	CASANI CLUB ORCH	214
Bye Bye Blues	AMBROSE & ORCH	(7 C18) 195
	NAT GONELLA & GEORGIANS	(61) 209
By Special Permission Of The Copyright Owners	SAVOY HOTEL ORPHEANS	205
By The River Sainte Marie*	ROY FOX & BAND	(C90) C163
California, Here I Come (Carroll Re-Calls The Tunes No.1)	CARROLL GIBBONS (Piano solo)	207
Canadian Capers*	HARRY ROY & ORCH	(156 159) C164
Can I Forget You?*	ROY FOX & ORCH	(41 C9 C141) 201
Can't Get Indiana Off My Mind	NAT GONELLA & NEW GEORGIANS	210
Can't Help Lovin' Dat Man*	RHYTHMIC EIGHT (B.FIRMAN)	C148
Canzonetta*	GERALDO & ORCH	202
Capri Caprice (Isle Of Capri)	NAT GONELLA & GEORGIANS	208
Caravan*	NAT GONELLA & GEORGIANS	210
	RONNIE MUNRO & ORCH With LARRY ADLER	C166
Carry Me Back To Old Virginny	GERALDO & ORCH	203
Cement Mixer	THE SQUADRONAIRES	(C107) C146
Change Partners*	JOE LOSS & BAND	(105 106) 217 C180
Charmaine (Silent Film Memories)	JOE LOSS & BAND	218
Cheek To Cheek* (Carroll Re-Calls The Tunes No.2)	CARROLL GIBBONS (Piano solo)	207
Cheerful Blues*	HARRY ROY'S TIGER-RAGAMUFFINS	(158) 225
Chelsea (From "London Suite")*	FATS WALLER (Piano solo)	C149 C150
Chinese Laundry Blues*	JACK HYLTON & ORCH/George Formby	(C61 C62 C98) C144 C154 C170
Cinderella Brown	SPIKE HUGHES & DANCE ORCH	C162
Clarinet Marmalade*	FRED ELIZALDE & MUSIC	(29 30 C45 C75) C142
Close Your Eyes (comp Bernice Petkere)*	RAY NOBLE & ORCH	(127 131 137 C17 C93) 220
Come Closer To Me	EDMUNDO ROS & RUMBA BAND	223
Come Happy Day*	C. GIBBONS & SAVOY HOTEL ORPHEANS	206
Come On Over	SAVOY ORPHEANS	226
Come With Me My Honey	EDMUNDO ROS & RUMBA BAND	(154) 223
Coming In On A Wing And A Prayer*	AMBROSE & ORCH	C146 C169
Concerto For Drums*	GERALDO & ORCH	203
Copenhagen	AMBROSE & ORCH	(12 C43) 196
	SAVOY ORPHEANS	(C56) 226
Coquette (comp J.Green,G.Kahn,C.Lombardo)*	VICTOR SILVESTER'S JIVE BAND	228
Cornsilk*	JOE LOSS & ORCH	219
Cowboy In Manhattan	HARRY ROY & ORCH	224

Cow Cow Boogie*	JOE LOSS & ORCH	219
Crazy Rhythm*	VICTOR SILVESTER'S JIVE BAND	228
	RAY STARITA & AMBASS.CLUB BAND(175)	C163
Cruising Down The River*	LOU PREAGER & ORCH	(C48) C176
Cry, Baby, Cry*	JOE LOSS & BAND	218
Cryin' For The Carolines *	AMBROSE & ORCH	(5 7) 195
Crying My Heart Out For You*	CHARLIE KUNZ & CASANI CLUB ORCH	(99) C174
Cuban Love Song*	EDMUNDO ROS & RUMBA BAND	223
Daddy*	JOE LOSS & ORCH	219
Dames	AMBROSE & ORCH	(12) 196
Dancing In The Dark*	AMBROSE & ORCH	(7) 195 C180
	SAVOY HOTEL ORPHEANS	(55 56 C12) 206
Dancing Time	SPIKE HUGHES & DANCE ORCH	C162
	OSCAR RABIN & STRICT TEMPO DANCE BAND	C174
Dancing With A Ghost	JACK JACKSON & ORCH	213
Danger Ahead (Piano Medley No.D84)	CHARLIE KUNZ (Piano) With rhythm acc	C172
Davenport Blues	MARK WHITE'S JAZZ CLUB	C143
Day In, Day Out	JACK HYLTON & ORCH	(90) 212
Dear Stranger	CASANI CLUB ORCH	214
Diane* (Reminiscing In Waltz Time)	CARROLL GIBBONS (Piano solo)	207
(Silent Film Memories)	JOE LOSS & BAND	218
Did My Heart Beat (Did I Fall In Love?)*	CASANI CLUB ORCH	214
Did You Ever Have a Feeling You're Flying?	ROY FOX & BAND	200
Did You Ever See A Dream Walking?*	CASANI CLUB ORCH	(98) 214
	RAY NOBLE & ORCH	(127 143 C85 C93) C153
Did You Go Down Lambeth Way?*	VICTOR SILVESTER & BALLROOM ORCH	227
Dinah*	BILLY COTTON & BAND	199
(Carroll Re-Calls The Tunes No.1)	CARROLL GIBBONS (Piano solo)	207
	STEPHANE GRAPPELLY & QUARTET	C151 C173
	SAVOY ORPHEANS	(C56) 226
Doan' You Grieve	SPIKE HUGHES & ORCH	C143
Do De O Do	JACK HYLTON & ORCH/George Formby	(C60 C62 C98) C145 C170
Do Do Do* (George Gershwin Suite)	LOUIS LEVY & MUSIC FROM MOVIES	215
Doggone, I've Done It*	CASANI CLUB ORCH	214
Do I Love You, Do I?*	C.GIBBONS & SAVOY HOTEL ORPHEANS	(C10) C156
Doin' The Uptown Lowdown	BILLY COTTON & BAND	199
Donde	GERALDO & GAUCHO TANGO ORCH	C165
Don't Change	LEW STONE & BAND	229
Don't Ever Pass Me By	VICTOR SILVESTER & BALLROOM ORCH	227
Don't Fence Me In	GERALDO & ORCH	(C10) C156
(Cole Porter Suite)	LOUIS LEVY & MUSIC FROM MOVIES	215
Don't Forget	JOE LOSS & BAND	216
Don't Let That Moon Get Away	JACK HYLTON & ORCH	(92) C180
Don't Say Goodbye*	VICTOR SILVESTER & BALLROOM ORCH	227
Don't Try Your Jive On Me*	FATS WALLER & CONTINENTAL RHYTHM	C149 C150
Don't You Cry When We Say Goodbye	JACK JACKSON & ORCH	213
Don't You Know I Care*	STEPHANE GRAPPELLY & QUARTET	C173
Dream	JOHNNY DENIS & NOVELTY SWINGTET	C172
Dreaming A Dream	RAY NOBLE & ORCH	(130 132 135 C19) 220
Dream Man (Make Me Dream Some More)	ROY FOX & BAND	200
Drowsy Blues	ROY FOX & BAND	(37) 200
Dust Off That Old Pianna	LEW STONE & BAND	(185) 230
Eadie Was A Lady	HARRY ROY & ORCH	C164
	LEW STONE & BAND	(179) 229
Early Talkie Memories, Part 2 (Medley)	JOE LOSS & BAND	218
East Of The Sun*	LEW STONE & BAND	(185) 230
Easy To Love*	BBC DANCE ORCH (HENRY HALL)	(C10) C156
Eccentric*	SAVOY ORPHEANS	(C49 C56) 226

Title	Artist	Ref.
Echoes Of The Jungle	MADAME TUSSAUD'S DANCE ORCH	197
Eeny Meeny Miney Mo	HARRY ROY & ORCH	225
'Leven Thirty Saturday Night*	AMBROSE & ORCH	(4 5 7 C75) 195
Embraceable You (George Gershwin Suite)	LOUIS LEVY & MUSIC FROM MOVIES	215
Ending With A Kiss*	JOE LOSS & BAND	216
Everybody's Swinging It Now	HARRY ROY & ORCH	225
Every Single Little Tingle Of My Heart	BILLY COTTON & BAND	199
Everything's In Rhythm With My Heart*	BBC DANCE ORCH (HENRY HALL)	211
Every Time I Look At You	HARRY ROY & ORCH	225
Exactly Like You* (Carroll Re-Calls The Tunes No.2)	CARROLL GIBBONS (Piano solo)	207
Experiment*	RAY NOBLE & ORCH	(126 134 143 C10) C156
Faint Harmony*	JACK JACKSON & ORCH	213
Fair And Warmer	ROY FOX & BAND	200
	RAY NOBLE & ORCH	(129 C14) 221
Faithful Forever	ORGAN, THE DANCE BAND & ME	231
"Falling For You" Selection	BILLY COTTON & BAND	198
Falling Leaves	GERALDO & SAVOY HOTEL ORCH	202
Fancy Our Meeting ("That's A Good Girl" Selection)	BILLY COTTON & BAND	198
Fan It	NAT GONELLA & GEORGIANS	209
	JOE LOSS & ORCH	219
Farewell Blues* (Medley)	HARRY ROY'S TIGER-RAGAMUFFINS	225
Fascinating Rhythm*	NAT GONELLA & GEORGIANS	210
Felix Kept On Walking (Silent Film Memories)	JOE LOSS & BAND	218
Fifty Million Robins Can't Be Wrong	ROY FOX & ORCH	(41) 201
Five Minutes More	THE SQUADRONAIRES	(174) C146
Five O'Clock Whistle	JOE LOSS & ORCH	219
	JAY WILBUR & BAND	(C105 C120) C175
Florianopolis	VICTOR SILVESTER & BALLROOM ORCH	227
For All That I Care*	JOE LOSS & ORCH	219
For All We know	C.GIBBONS & SAVOY HOTEL ORPHEANS	205 C163
Forty-Second Street* ("42nd Street" Film Selection)	BILLY COTTON & BAND	198
"Forty-Second Street" Film Selection*	BILLY COTTON & BAND	198
For You Madonna	JOE LOSS & ORCH	216
Freckle Face, You're Beautiful*	RAY NOBLE & ORCH	(130) 221
Georgia On My Mind*	NAT GONELLA (With Instr.Acc.)	(59 C45 C80 C115) C142
Georgia Rockin' Chair*	NAT GONELLA & GEORGIANS	208
Gershwin (George) Suite	LOUIS LEVY & MUSIC FROM MOVIES	215
Gertie The Girl With The Gong	HARRY ROY & ORCH	224
Get Happy	LEW STONE & STONECRACKERS	(183) C174
Get Hot	NAT GONELLA & GEORGIANS	209
Get Rhythm In Your Feet	VICTOR SILVESTER & BALLROOM ORCH	227
Getting Nowhere	GERALDO & ORCH	(53) 204
Girls Were Made To Love And Kiss	JACK HYLTON & ORCH	212
Gnat Jump	NAT GONELLA & GEORGIANS	(C100 C125) C174
Gonna Wed That Girl O'Mine	NAT GONELLA & GEOGIANS	208
Goodbye Blues* (Medley)	HARRY ROY'S TIGER-RAGAMUFFINS	225
Good Little, Bad Little You	NEW MAYFAIR DANCE O (C.GIBBONS)(C121)	C163
Goodnight, Lovely Little Lady*	JACK JACKSON & ORCH	213
Goodnight Sweetheart*	NEW MAYFAIR DANCE ORCH (RAY NOBLE)	(118 133 139 140 C84) 220 C153 C177
Goodnight Vienna*	R.NOBLE & NEW MAYFIAR O	(121 136) 220
Gosh, I Must Be Falling In Love	LEW STONE & BAND	229
Grinzing*	RAY NOBLE & ORCH	(130 138) 220
Guilty*	JACK PAYNE & BBC DANCE ORCH	222

If A Grey-Haired Lady Says 'How's Yer Father?'	AMBROSE & ORCH	C160
I Faw Down And Go Boom	JACK PAYNE & BBC DANCE ORCH	222 C154
If I Could Be With You One Hour Tonight*	JACK PAYNE & BBC DANCE ORCH	(146) 222
If I Could Paint A Memory	ORGAN, THE DANCE BAND & ME	231
If I Had A Million Dollars	AMBROSE & ORCH	196
If I Had A Talking Picture Of You* (Early Talkie Memories)	JOE LOSS & BAND	218
If I Had My Way*	AMBROSE & ORCH	C169
If I Love Again*	AMBROSE & ORCH	196
If I Only Had Wings*	GERALDO & SAVOY HOTEL ORCH	202
If I Should Fall In Love Again*	JOE LOSS & ORCH	219
	VICTOR SILVESTER & BALLROOM ORCH	227
If It Rains, Who Cares?	ROY FOX & ORCH	(41) 201
If Love Were All*	AMBROSE & ORCH	194
If The Moon Turns Green*	ROY FOX & BAND	200
If You Don't Want The Goods, Don't Maul 'Em	JACK HYLTON & ORCH/George Formby	(C60 C62) C170
I Get A Kick Out Of You* (Cole Porter Suite)	LOUIS LEVY & MUSIC FROM MOVIES	215
	HARRY ROY & ORCH	(C10) C156
I Get Along Without You Very Well*	LEW STONE & BAND	(178) C176
I Got Rhythm*	HATCHETT'S SWINGTETTE	(70) C173
(George Gershwin Suite)	LOUIS LEVY & MUSIC FROM MOVIES	215
	ROLAND PEACHEY & ROYAL HAWAIIANS	C174
I Got The Sun In The Morning	EDMUNDO ROS & RUMBA BAND	223
I Guess I'll Have To Dream The Rest	LEW STONE & BAND	C175
I Hadn't Anyone Till You*	GERALDO & ORCH	202
I Have Eyes*	CARROLL GIBBONS & SAVOY HOTEL ORPHEANS	206
I Hear A Rhapsody*	LEW STONE & BAND	C175
I Hum A Waltz	VICTOR SILVESTER & BALLROOM ORCH	227
I Lay Me Down To Sleep	LEW STONE & MONSEIGNEUR BAND	229
I Like Riding On A Choo Choo	BILLY TERNENT & ORCH	(186) C172
I Like To Do Things For You	SPIKE HUGHES & DANCE ORCH	C162
I'll Buy That Dream	LEW STONE & NOVA-TONES	(C104) C174
I'll Dance At Your Wedding	JACK WHITE & ORCH	C174
I'll Do My Best To Make You Happy*	RAY NOBLE & NEW MAYFAIR DANCE ORCH	(122 132 135 139) 220
I'll Make Up For Everything (Piano Medley No. D84)	CHARLIE KUNZ (Piano) with rhythm acc	C172
I'll Never Say "Never Again" Again*	BILLY COTTON & BAND	(24) 199
	JACK HYLTON & ORCH	(93) 212
I'll Pray For You	VICTOR SILVESTER & BALLROOM ORCH	227
I'll See You Again*	AMBROSE & ORCH	194
(Reminiscing In Waltz Time)	CARROLL GIBBONS (Piano solo)	207
I'll See You In My Dreams* (Carroll Re-Calls The Tunes No.3)	CARROLL GIBBONS (Piano solo)	207
I'll String Along With You*	BBC DANCE ORCH (HENRY HALL)	211
	ROY FOX & BAND	200
	RAY NOBLE & ORCH	(129 131 C14 C84 C93) 220
I Love You Truly	JOE LOSS & BAND	216
	RAY NOBLE & ORCH	(129 C23) C153
	LEW STONE & BAND	(180 C22) 229
I'm A Ding Dong Daddy	HARRY ROY'S TIGER-RAGAMUFIFNS	225
I'm Coming, Virginia*	VICTOR SILVESTER'S JIVE BAND	228
I'm Confessin' (That I Love You)*	STEPHANE GRAPPELLY & QUARTET	C173
	NAT GONELLA & GEORGIANS	209 210
I'm Crazy For You	EDMUNDO ROS & CUBAN ORCH	223
I'm Going Back To Himazaz	DEBROY SOMER'S BAND	C154
I'm Going To Get Lit-Up*	BILLY COTTON & BAND	C146
	C.GIBBONS & SAVOY HOTEL ORPHEANS	(56) 206
I'm Gonna Lock My Heart And Throw Away The Key*	JOE LOSS & BAND	(105 C24) 217
I'm Gonna Wash My Hands Of You*	AMBROSE & ORCH	(C103) C159

It's Easy To Remember*	LEW STONE & BAND	(185) 230
It's Foolish But It's Fun*	ORGAN, THE DANCE BAND & ME	231
	ROYAL AIR FORCE DANCE ORCH	C169
It's Gonna Be You	SAVOY HOTEL ORPHEANS	205
It's Only A Paper Moon	BILLY COTTON & BAND	198
It's The Girl	BILLY COTTON & BAND	(21) C163
I've Got A Feeling I'm Falling* (Tribute To Fats Waller)	CARROLL GIBBONS (Piano solo)	207
I've Got A Lovely Bunch Of Coconuts*	BILLY COTTON & BAND	C146
I've Got An Invitation To A Dance*	ROY FOX & BAND	200
I've Got My Eyes On You*	GERALDO & SAVOY HOTEL ORCH	202
	C.GIBBONS & SAVOY HOTEL ORPHEANS(C10)	C156
I've Got My Love To Keep Me Warm*	ROY FOX & ORCH	(41) 201
	RONNIE MUNRO & ORCH With LARRY ADLER	C166
I've Got Sixpence*	BILLY COTTON & BAND	(C105) C167
I've Got To Sing A Torch Song	RAY NOBLE & ORCH	(126 C85) 220
I've Got You Under My Skin	BBC DANCE ORCH (HENRY HALL)	(C10) C156
(Cole Porter Suite)	LOUIS LEVY & MUSIC FROM MOVIES	215
	RONNIE MUNRO & ORCH With LARRY ADLER	C166
I've Had My Moments*	BILLY COTTON & BAND	199
I Want The Waiter	CARROLL GIBBONS (Piano & Vocal)	207
I Want To Be Happy*	NAT GONELLA & GEORGIANS	(60) 209
I Was In The Mood*	HARRY ROY & ORCH	224
I Was True*	HENRY HALL & GLENEAGLES HOTEL BAND	C174
I Was Watching A Man Paint A Fence	GERALDO & SAVOY HOTEL ORCH	202
I Wish I Could Fish	GERALDO & ORCH	203
I Wish I Knew A Bigger Word For Love	SAVOY HOTEL ORPHEANS	205
I Wish I Were Twins*	VICTOR SILVESTER'S JIVE BAND	228
I Won't Dance*	LEW STONE & BAND	(185) 230
Japanese Sandman*	NAT GONELLA & GEORGIANS	208 210
Jazz Cocktail	MADAME TUSSAUD'S DANCE ORCH	197
Jazz Me Blues*	HARRY ROY'S TIGER-RAGAMUFFINS	225
Jealous	NAT GONELLA & GEORGIANS	208
(Fox-Trot Medley)	HARRY ROY'S TIGER-RAGAMUFFINS	225
Jeepers Creepers*	JACK HYLTON & ORCH	(90) 212
Jig Time*	NAT GONELLA & GEORGIANS	208
Jig Walk*	SAVOY ORPHEANS	226
Jingle Bells	P.SCALA'S BANJO & ACC.BAND (H.BIDGOOD)	C171
Jive Bomber	STEPHANE GRAPPELLY & QUARTET	C151 C173
Jungle Drums	ROY FOX & BAND	(37) 200
Just So You'll Remember*	BBC DANCE ORCH (HENRY HALL)	211
Just You, Just Me*	AMBROSE & ORCH	194
Kalua	SPIKE HUGHES & DANCE ORCH	(C49) C162
Keep An Eye On Your Heart*	ROYAL AIR FORCE DANCE ORCH	(C104) C169
Keepin' Out Of Mischief Now* (Tribute To Fats Waller)	CARROLL GIBBONS (Piano solo)	207
Kicking The Gong Around*	NAT GONELLA & GEORGIANS	209
Kiss And Make Up	THE PICCADILLY PLAYERS	(C29) C148
Kiss By Kiss*	SAVOY HOTEL ORPHEANS	(C117) 205
Kiss Me Again (Reminiscing In Waltz Time)	CARROLL GIBBONS (Piano solo)	207
Kiss Me, Dear*	JACK JACKSON & ORCH	213 C163
Knock Knock (Harry Roy Stage Show)	HARRY ROY & ORCH	225
La Cucaracha*	AMBROSE & ORCH	C160
	BILLY COTTON & BAND	199
La Di Da Di Da*	AMBROSE & ORCH	C160
	THE BARNSTORMERS	C174
Lady Be Good*	NAT GONELLA & GEORGIANS	209
	HATCHETT'S SWINGTETTE	(70) C173

Lady Of Spain*	JACK PAYNE & BBC DANCE ORCH	222
Lazybones*	CASANI CLUB ORCH	214
	SYDNEY KYTE & PICCADILLY HOTEL BAND	C174
Lazy Day*	NEW MAYFAIR DANCE ORCH (RAY NOBLE)	(119 132 138 140 C17) 220
	JACK PAYNE & BBC DANCE ORCH	(145) 222
Lazy Rhythm*	NAT GONELLA & GEORGIANS	209
Lazy River	NAT GONELLA & GEORGIANS	(C49) 208
Learn To Croon*	CASANI CLUB ORCH	(98) 214
Leave The Rest To Nature	ROY FOX & BAND	C160
Leicester Square Rag*	HARRY ROY & ORCH	(162) C167
Let Him Go, Let Him Tarry*	JOE LOSS & ORCH	C167
Let It Snow, Let It Snow, Let It Snow	LEW STONE & NOVA-TONES	(183) C146
Let's All Sing Like The Birdies Sing*	JACK PAYNE & BAND	C154
Let's Be Buddies	HARRY ROY & BAND	(C10) C156
Let's Be Sensible	CARROLL GIBBONS (Piano solo)	(56) 206
Let's Break The Good News	ORGAN, THE DANCE BAND & ME	231
Let's Call It A Day	HARRY ROY & ORCH/Leslie Hutchinson	(C124) C164
Let's Dance At The Make Believe Ballroom	JOE LOSS & BAND	(105 107) 217
Let's Do It*	JACK HYLTON & ORCH	(C10) C156
(Cole Porter Suite)	LOUIS LEVY & MUSIC FROM MOVIES	215
Let's Face The Music And Dance*	ROY FOX & ORCH	(41) 201 C180
Let's Fall In Love	JOE LOSS & BAND	(C80 C103) 216
Let's Have A Jubilee*	HARRY ROY & ORCH	224
Let's Put Out The Lights And Go To Sleep*	AMBROSE & ORCH	(7 C139) 195
Let's Sit This One Out	CASANI CLUB ORCH	(98) 214
Let The Curtain Come Down	JOE LOSS & ORCH	219
Let The People Sing*	JACK HYLTON & ORCH	212
Levi's Monkey Mike	JACK HYLTON & ORCH/George Formby	(C60) C170
Life Begins When You're In Love*	AMBROSE & ORCH	(15) C160
Life Of The Party	GERALDO & ORCH	203
Lightning	MADAME TUSSAUD'S DANCE ORCH	197
Like Taking Candy From A Baby	HARRY ROY & ORCH	(157) C163
Limehouse (From "London Suite")*	FATS WALLER (Piano solo)	C149 C150
Limehouse Blues*	AMBROSE & ORCH	(11 C81 C112) C176
Little Brown Baby	SAVOY ORPHEANS	226
Little Jack Frost Get Lost	GERALDO & ORCH	(53) 203
Little Lady Make Believe*	VICTOR SILVESTER & BALLROOM ORCH	227
Little Sir Echo*	JOE LOSS & BAND	(105 106) 217
Little Valley In The Mountains*	BBC DANCE ORCH (HENRY HALL)	211
Liza (All The Clouds'll Roll Away)	STEPHANE GRAPPELLY & QUINTET	C173
London On A Rainy Night*	AMBROSE & ORCH	196
	HARRY ROY & ORCH	224
London Suite*	FATS WALLER (Piano solos)	C149 C150
Lonely Feet*	JACK JACKSON & ORCH	213
Lonely Serenade	LEW STONE & BAND	C175
Looking On The Bright Side Of Life	RAY NOBLE & NEW MAYFAIR D.O.	(122 133) C153
Lost In A Fog*	AMBROSE & ORCH	196
Louise*	AMBROSE & ORCH	194
Louisiana Lullaby	HARRY ROY & ORCH	(157) 224
Love And A Dime	HARRY ROY & ORCH	224
Love And Learn	ROY FOX & ORCH	(41) 201
Love For Sale	JACK HYLTON & ORCH	(C10) C156
	JACK PAYNE & BBC DANCE ORCH	C155
Love In Bloom*	BBC DANCE ORCH (HENRY HALL)	211
Love Is A Dancing Thing*	ROY FOX & ORCH	(40 41) 201
Love Is A Dreamer	AMBROSE & ORCH	194
Love Is The Sweetest Thing*	RAY NOBLE & NEW MAYFAIR DANCE ORCH	(122 133 139 C23 C84) 220 C153
Love Letters In The Sand*	JACK PAYNE & BBC DANCE ORCH	222
Love Live Forever And Rule My heart	JACK HYLTON & ORCH	212
Love Makes The World Go Round*	ORGAN, THE DANCE BAND & ME	231

Love Me, Or Leave Me*	VICTOR SILVESTER'S JIVE BAND	228
Lover	HARRY ROY & ORCH/Leslie Hutchinson	(C110 C124) C164
Lover's Lullaby	ROYAL AIR FORCE DANCE ORCH	C169
Love Walked In* (George Gershwin Suite)	LOUIS LEVY & MUSIC FROM MOVIES	215
Lucky Me, Lovable You	AMBROSE & ORCH	194
Lullaby Of Broadway* (Early Talkie Memories)	JOE LOSS & BAND	218
Madam-Ah! La Marquise-Ah!*	JOE LOSS & BAND	(105) 217
Ma, I Miss Your Apple Pie*	BILLY COTTON & BAND	C167
Mama Don't Allow It	NAT GONELLA & GEORGIANS	209
Mama Don't Want No Peas And Rice And Coconut Oil	HARRY ROY & ORCH	C164
Managua Nicaragua	EDMUNDO ROS & RUMBA BAND	223
Manana (Is Soon Enough For Me)	EDMUNDO ROS & RUMBA BAND	(154) 223 C146
Manhattan Holiday*	CARROLL GIBBONS (Piano solo)	207
Maracas*	AMBROSE & ORCH	196
Marcheta (Reminiscing In Waltz Time)	CARROLL GIBBONS (Piano solo)	207
Margie*	SPIKE HUGHES & DANCE ORCH	C162
Maria From Bahia	EDMUNDO ROS & RUMBA BAND	223
Mary Lou	CARROLL GIBBONS & SAVOY HOTEL ORPHEANS	C167
Maybe It's Because I Love You Too Much*	RAY NOBLE & ORCH	(125 132 135 C17) 220
Maybe It's Me	JACK HYLTON & ORCH	C158
May I?*	CARROLL GIBBONS & SAVOY HOTEL ORPHEANS	205
Me And My Girl*	RONNIE MUNRO & ORCH	(C127) C180
Memories Live Longer Than Dreams*	JOE LOSS & ORCH	219
Memories Of Hours Spent With You	CASANI CLUB ORCH	214
Memories Of You* (Medley)	HARRY ROY'S TIGER-RAGAMUFFINS	225
Midnight And The Stars And You	RAY NOBLE & ORCH	(128 133) 221
Miss Elizabeth Brown*	JACK PAYNE & BBC DANCE ORCH	222
Miss Otis Regrets*	HARRY ROY & ORCH	(C10) C156
Mood Indigo*	BILLY COTTON & BAND	198
	MADAME TUSSAUD'S DANCE ORCH	197
Moonbeams Dance*	CARROLL GIBBONS (Piano solo)	207
Moonglow*	LOUIS DE VRIES & RHYTHM BOYS	C160
Moonlight Avenue*	OSCAR RABIN & BAND	C169
	VICTOR SILVESTER & BALLROOM ORCH	227
Moon Over Miami*	AL COLLINS & ORCH	C174
Moonstruck*	CASANI CLUB ORCH	(98) 214
More And More*	AMBROSE & ORCH	C169
Mountain Greenery*	TED HEATH & MUSIC	C168
Mr. Reynard's Nightmare*	AMBROSE & ORCH	(10) C160
Mrs. Bartholomew ("Falling For You" Sel)	BILLY COTTON & BAND	198
Muddy Water* (Medley)	HARRY ROY'S TIGER-RAGAMUFFINS	225
Murder	NAT GONELLA & GEORGIANS	(C100 C125) C172
Music, Maestro, Please*	VICTOR SILVESTER & BALLROOM ORCH	227
	FATS WALLER & CONTINENTAL RHYTHM	C149 C150
My Baby Just Cares For Me*	JACK PAYNE & BBC DANCE ORCH	(146) 222 C163
My Bluebird's Singing The Blues	MADAME TUSSAUD'S DANCE ORCH	197
My Blue Heaven* (Silent Film Memories)	JOE LOSS & BAND	218
My Darling	BBC DANCE ORCH (HENRY HALL)	211
My Hat's On The Side Of My Head*	RAY NOBLE & ORCH	(127 136) 221
	HARRY ROY & ORCH	224
My Belongs To Daddy*	JACK HYLTON & ORCH	(C10) C156
(Cole Porter Suite)	LOUIS LEVY & MUSIC FROM MOVIES	215
My Heart's To Let*	LEW STONE & MONSEIGNEUR BAND	C174
My Heart Stood Still*	GERALDO & CONCERT ORCH	204
My Heart Tells Me*	STEPHANE GRAPPELLY & QUARTET	C173
Me Ideal*	GERALDO & ORCH	203
My Love Is Only For You	PRIMO SCALA'S ACCORDEON BD (H.BIDGOOD)	C146
My Love Parade	AMBROSE & ORCH	194
My Melancholy Baby*	VICTOR SILVESTER'S JIVE BAND	228
My Old Dog	LEW STONE & BAND	(185) 230

My Pet*	SYD ROY'S LYRICALS	C164
My Prayer*	JACK HYLTON & ORCH	(90 91) 212
My Romance*	AMBROSE & ORCH	C160
My Silent Love	SAVOY HOTEL ORPHEANS (C.GIBBONS)	(55) C163
My Song Goes Round The World	RAY NOBLE & ORCH	(127 143) C153
My Sweeter Than Sweet	AMBROSE & ORCH	194
My Wubba Dolly*	AMBROSE & ORCH	C169
	OSCAR RABIN & BAND	
Nagasaki*	NAT GONELLA & GEORGIANS	(C14) 210
Nattering Around	NAT TEMPLE & CLUB ROYAL ORCH	(C125) C174
Nature Boy	GERALDO & CONCERT ORCH	204
Nevertheless*	AMBROSE & ORCH	(5 6) C160
Nice People	JACK HYLTON & ORCH	212
Night And Day* (Cole Porter Suite)	LOUIS LEVY & MUSIC FROM MOVIES	215
	RONNIE MUNRO & ORCH With LARRY ADLER	C166
	HARRY ROY & ORCH	(C10) C156
Night Owl	BILLY COTTON & BAND	198
Noel Brings The Swing	STEPHANE GRAPPELLY & MUSICIANS	(C151) C173
No, Mama, No!*	JOE LOSS & ORCH	219
No Moon, No Stars, Just You	HARRY ROY & ORCH	224
No! No'. A Thousand Times No	AMBROSE & ORCH	(C102) C159
No One Else Will Do	STEPHANE GRAPPELLY & QUARTET	C173
Now That We're Sweethearts Again	JACK JACKSON & ORCH	213
Number Ten Lullaby Lane	LEW STONE & BAND	C175
Oceans Of Time*	CARROLL GIBBONS & SAVOY HOTEL ORPHS	205
Of Thee I Sing (George Gershwin Suite)	LOUIS LEVY & MUSIC FROM MOVIES	215
Oh! By Jingo (Oh! By Gee)*	HATCHETT'S SWINGTETTE	(70) C173
Oh! Eva (Ain't You Coming Out Tonight?)*	SAVOY ORPHEANS	(C56) 226
Oh! Johnny, Oh Johnny, Oh!	HATCHETT'S SWINGTETTE	C173
	JOE LOSS & BAND	218
Oh Me, Oh My (Carroll Re-Calls The Tunes No. 2)	CARROLL GIBBONS (Piano solo)	207
Oh, My Darling	GERALDO & ORCH	(53) 203
Oh! Peter (You're So Nice)	NAT GONELLA & GEORGIANS	208
Oh! That Sweet In Suite 16	SAVOY ORPHEANS	(C56) 226
Oh, You Crazy Moon	JOE LOSS & BAND	218
Okay Toots*	AMBROSE & ORCH	C160
Old Fashioned Sweethearts	MADAME TUSSAUD'S DANCE ORCH	197
Old Man Blues	MADAME TUSSAUD'S DANCE ORCH	197
Ol' Man Mose	NAT GONELLA & GEORGIANS	(61) 209
Old Man River*	NAT GONELLA & GEORGIANS	209
Ole Faithful*	JACK JACKSON & ORCH	213
	JOE LOSS & BAND	216
On A Steamer Coming Over*	BBC DANCE ORCH (HENRY HALL)	211
One Hour With You*	SAVOY HOTEL ORPHEANS	205
One Little Word Led To Another	BILLY COTTON & BAND	199
One Meat Ball	NAT GONELLA & GEORGIANS	(C104) C167 C174
One Morning In May*	ROY FOX & BAND	200
	CARROLL GIBBONS & SAVOY HOTEL ORPHEANS	205
	JOE LOSS & BAND	(C115) 216
Only Make Believe	GERALDO & ORCH	203
On The Air*	CARROLL GIBBONS & BOY FRIENDS	(56) 206
On The Good Ship Lollipop*	CASANI CLUB ORCH	(99) 214
On The Sentimental Side*	GERALDO & ORCH	202
On The Sunny Side Of The Street*	JACK HARRIS & ORCH	(C80) C174
	VICTOR SILVESTER & BALLROOM ORCH	227
Ooo-La-La ("That's A Good Girl" Seln)	BILLY COTTON & BAND	198
Organ Grinder's Swing*	AMBROSE & ORCH	C160
Our Love Affair*	GERALDO & SAVOY HOTEL ORCH	202
Out In The Cold Again	ROY FOX & BAND	200
Out Of Nowhere*	ROYAL AIR FORCE DANCE ORCH	(C104) C169
Out Of The Dawn*	JACK PAYNE & BBC DANCE ORCH	222

Over My Shoulder*	JOE LOSS & BAND	(105) 217
Over On The Sunny Side	RAY NOBLE & ORCH	(128) 221
Painting The Clouds With Sunshine*	JACK HYLTON & ORCH	(82 85 C19 C21) C152
Papa's In Bed With His Breeches On	HATCHETT'S SWINGTETTE	C172
Paradise Isle	FELIX MENDELSSOHN & HAWAIIAN SER.	C167
Pardon Me, Pretty Baby*	VICTOR SILVESTER'S JIVE BAND	228
Penny Serenade*	JOE LOSS & BAND	218
Pent Up In A Penthouse	FATS WALLER & CONTINENTAL RHYTHM	C149 C150
Piano Madness* (Harry Roy Stage Show)	HARRY ROY & ORCH	225
Piano Medley No.D84	CHARLIE KUNZ (Piano) with rhythm acc	C172
Piccadilly (From "London Suite")*	FATS WALLER (Piano solo)	C149 C150
Piccolo Pete*	AMBROSE & ORCH	194
Pidgin' English Hula	NAT GONELLA & GEORGIANS	208
Playmates*	HATCHETT'S SWINGTETTE	C173
Play, Orchestra, Play	ROY FOX & ORCH	(41) 201
Play to Me Gypsy*	JACK JACKSON & ORCH	213 C163
Please*	RAY NOBLE & ORCH	(123) C153
Please Be Kind	JOE LOSS & BAND	(105 106) 217
Please Do It Again*	VICTOR SILVESTER'S JIVE BAND	228
Poor Butterfly*	SPIKE HUGHES & DANCE ORCH	C162
(Fox-Trot Medley)	HARRY ROY'S TIGER-RAGAMUFFINS	225
	VICTOR SILVESTER'S JIVE BAND	228
Poor Little Angeline* (Palais Glide Med)	JOE LOSS & BAND	218
Porter (Cole) Suite	LOUIS LEVY & MUSIC FROM MOVIES	215
Power House	AMBROSE & ORCH	C160
Pu-Leeze! Mister Hemingway	AMBROSE & ORCH	(7) 195 C181
Queer Street	GERALDO & ORCH	203
Quien No Llora No Mama	EDMUNDO ROS & RUMBA BAND	C174
Ragtime Cowboy Joe	GERALDO & ORCH	(50) 202
	GERALDO & ORCH (radio transcr.)	203
Rain* (Medley)	HARRY ROY'S TIGER-RAGAMUFFINS	225
Rain, Rain, Go Away	LEW STONE & MONSEIGNEUR BAND	(178) 229
Ramona* (Silent Film Memories)	JOE LOSS & BAND	218
Reflections On The Water	SQUADRONAIRES/Sam Browne	C172
Rehearsing A Lullaby	AMBROSE & ORCH	C174
Remember Me?*	JOE LOSS & BAND	218
Rhapsody In Blue, Parts 1 & 2	BILLY COTTON & BAND	198
	C.GIBBONS & SAVOY HO.ORPH/LARRY ADLER	C166
Rhapsody In Rhythm	RAY STARITA & AMBASS CLUB BAND	(175) C148
Rhythmatitis	JACK PAYNE & BBC DANCE ORCH	222
Rhythm Mad	BILLY COTTON & BAND	199
Ridin' High	GERALDO & SAVOY HOTEL ORCH	(C10) C156
	SID PHILLIPS' QUINTET	C174
Rio De Janeiro	EDMUNDO ROS & RUMBA BAND	223
River Stay 'Way From My Door*	JACK PAYNE & BBC DANCE ORCH	222
Roadhouse Revels ("Bandwaggon" Film Sel)	JACK HYLTON & ORCH	212
Roaming	BBC DANCE ORCH (HENRY HALL)	211
	CASANI CLUB ORCH	214
Rock And Roll	HARRY ROY & ORCH	(157) C164
Rockin' In Rhythm	MADAME TUSSAUD'S DANCE ORCH	(C49) 197
Rockin' Through Dixie	GERALDO & ORCH	204
Roll Away, Clouds	AMBROSE & ORCH	194
Roll Me Over	PRIMO SCALA'S ACCORDEON BAND	C146
Roll Up The Carpet*	MADAME TUSSAUD'S DANCE ORCH	197
Room Five-Hundred-And-Four*	C.GIBBONS & SAVOY HOTEL ORPHS	(56 C37) 206
	BILLY MAYERL (Piano solo)	C146
Rosalie*	CARROLL GIBBONS & SAVOY HOTEL ORPHEANS	C155
(Carroll Re-Calls The Tunes No.3)	CARROLL GIBBONS (Piano solo)	207

Somebody Loves Me*		
(Carroll Re-Calls The Tunes No.3)	CARROLL GIBBONS (Piano solo)	207
(George Gershwin Suite)	LOUIS LEVY & MUSIC FROM MOVIES	215
Somebody Stole My Gal*	BILLY COTTON & BAND	198 199
(Harry Roy Stage Show)	HARRY ROY & ORCH	(162) 225
Someday Sweetheart*	STEPHANE GRAPPELLY & QUARTET	C173
	HARRY ROY'S TIGER-RAGAMUFFINS	225
Some Of These Days*	BILLY COTTON & BAND	199
	JACK HYLTON & ORCH	(87 C112) C143
Someone*	NIGHT CLUB KINGS (RAY NOBLE)	(C70) C148
Someone Stole Gabriel's Horn	NAT GONELLA & GEORGIANS	(61) 209
Someone To Care For	LEW STONE & MONSEIGNEUR BAND	229
Someone To Watch Over Me*		
(George Gershwin Suite)	LOUIS LEVY & MUSIC FROM MOVIES	215
Sometimes (comp G. Kahn, C. Lombardo)	OSCAR RABIN & BAND	C169
Song Without Words	RAY NOBLE & ORCH	(127) 221
Soon (comp Fitzgerald, Lisbona)	ROY FOX & BAND	200
	JACK JACKSON & ORCH	(96) 213
	JOE LOSS & BAND	216
Sophisticated Lady*	BILLY COTTON & BAND	199
	NAT GONELLA & GEORGIANS	208
	MADAME TUSSAUD'S DANCE ORCH	197
So Rare*	JOE LOSS & BAND	(105 106) 217
South American Way*	GERALDO & ORCH	(C99) 203
South America Take It Away	EDMUNDO ROS & RUMBA BAND	223
South Of Pago Pago	VICTOR SILVESTER & BALLROOM ORCH	227
South Sea Island Magic	ROY FOX & ORCH	(41) 201
Speak To Me Of Love		
(Reminiscing In Waltz Time)	CARROLL GIBBONS (Piano solo)	207
Squareface	NAT GONELLA & GEORGIANS	(60) 208
Stage Coach	ERIC WINSTONE & BAND	(C38 C48) C167
Stardust*	AMBROSE & ORCH	(7) 195
	STEPHANE GRAPPELLY & QUINTET	C151
	TOMMY KINSMAN & DANCE BAND	C174
Star Eyes	STEPHANE GRAPPELLY & QUARTET	C173
Stars Fell On Alabama*	AMBROSE & ORCH	196
	JOE LOSS & BAND	(C102) 216
Stars Over Devon	HARRY ROY & ORCH	224
Static Strut	SAVOY ORPHEANS	226
Stay As Sweet As You Are*	LEW STONE & BAND	(185) 230
Stay Out Of The South	SYD ROY'S LYRICALS	C164
Stephane's Blues	STEPHANE GRAPPELLY & MUSICIANS	C173
Stephane's Tune	STEPHANE GRAPPELLY & MUSICIANS	C173
Stevedore Stomp	MADAME TUSSAUD'S DANCE ORCH	197
St. Louis Blues*	BILLY COTTON & BAND	(24 25) 198
	LOUIS DE VRIES & RHYTHM BOYS	C160
	JIMMY DORSEY Acc by SPIKE HUGHES & THREE BLIND MICE	(C46) C162
(Harry Roy Stage Show)	HARRY ROY & ORCH	225
Stomping At The Savoy	VICTOR SILVESTER'S JIVE BAND	228
Stomp Off, Let's go	SAVOY ORPHEANS	226
Stomp Your Feet	FRED ELIZALDE & MUSIC	(29 30 C75) C143
Stormy Weather*		
(Carroll Re-Calls The Tunes No.2)	CARROLL GIBBONS (Piano solo)	207
	GEORGE SCOTT WOOD & ORCH With L.ALDER	C166
Straighten Up And Fly Right	VICTOR SILVESTER'S JIVE BAND	227
Straight From The Shoulder*	LEW STONE & BAND	(C83) 229
Stratton Street Strut	DANNY POLO & SWING STARS	(C45 C72) C143
Streamline Strut*	AMBROSE & ORCH	(10) C160
Strike Up The Band*		
(George Gershwin Suite)	LOUIS LEVY & MUSIC FROM MOVIES	215
Strut Miss Lizzie*	SID PHILLIPS' QUINTET	C143
Summer Rain	CARROLL GIBBONS (Piano solo)	207
Sunny Skies*	ARCADIANS DANCE ORCH (B.FIRMAN)	C148

Supposin' (comp Evans,Butler,Damerell)	SYDNEY LIPTON & GROS. HSE. ORCH	(104) C174
Swaller Tail Coat	ROY FOX & BAND	200
Swanee*	STANLEY BLACK & MODERNISTS	C160
(George Gershwin Suite)	LOUIS LEVY & MUSIC FROM MOVIES	215
Sweep* ("Falling For You" Selection)	BILLY COTTON & BAND	198
Sweet And Hot*	NAT GONELLA & GEORGIANS	(60) 208
Sweet And Lovely*	SAVOY HOTEL ORPHEANS (C.GIBBONS)	(54 C51 C85 C93) C153
Sweet Georgia Brown*	VICTOR SILVESTER'S JIVE BAND	227
Sweetheart*	BILLY COTTON & BAND	199
Sweetheart Of All My Dreams	MIFF FERRIE & FERRYMEN	C174
Sweet Little Sweetheart	JOE LOSS & ORCH	219
Sweet Music Man	NAT GONELLA & GEORGIANS	209
Sweet Sixteen And Never Been Kissed	BLUE MOUNTAINEERS	(C100) C160
Sweet Sue, Just You*	GERALDO & SAVOY HOTEL ORCH	202
(Carroll Re-Calls The Tunes No.1)	CARROLL GIBBONS (Piano solo)	207
	STEPHANE GRAPPELLY & MUSICIANS	C151 C173
	JOE LOSS & BAND	(105 106) 217
	JACK PAYNE & BBC DANCE ORCH	(146) 222
Swing*	HARRY ROY & ORCH	225
Swinging To Those Lies	NAT GONELLA & GEORGIANS	209
Swinging With The Wind	GERALDO & ORCH	203
Swing Is In The Air*	AMBROSE & ORCH	(15) C160
Swingy Little Thingy*	HARRY ROY & ORCH	224
'S Wonderful*	AMBROSE & ORCH	194
(George Gershwin Suite)	LOUIS LEVY & MUSIC FROM MOVIES	215
Take It Away	EDMUNDO ROS & RUMBA BAND	223
Taking A Chance On Love*	GERALDO & ORCH	202
Tarantula	AMBROSE & ORCH	C160
Tenement Symphony	GERALDO & ORCH	(53) 203
Thanks*	BBC DANCE ORCH (HENRY HALL)	211
	RAY NOBLE & ORCH	(127 143) C153
	LEW STONE & BAND	(178 C88) 229
That Lovely Week-End*	JOE LOSS & ORCH	(C47) 219
That Old Black Magic	STEPHANE GRAPPELLY & QUINTET	C173
"That's A Good Girl" Selection	BILLY COTTON & BAND	198
That's Another Scottish Story	BBC DANCE ORCH (HENRY HALL)	211
That's A-Plenty*	RHYTHM MANIACS (P.LEWIS)	(C49) C148
	HARRY ROY'S TIGER-RAGAMUFFINS	225
That's My Hap-Hap-Happiness	SAVOY ORPHEANS	226
That's What Life Is Made Of*	RAY NOBLE & ORCH	(125 134 139 C51) 221
The Ache In My Heart	JACK JACKSON & ORCH	213
The Beat O' My Heart*	CARROLL GIBBONS & SAVOY HOTEL ORPHEANS	205
	HARRY ROY & ORCH	(157) 224
The Blue Room*	SAVOY ORPHEANS	C158
The Bouncing Ball	LEW STONE & BAND	(185) 230
The Chestnut Tree	JOE LOSS & BAND	218
The Coffee Song	EDMUNDO ROS & RUMBA BAND	223 C146
The Continental*	JOE LOSS & BAND	216
The Cookhouse Serenade	AMBROSE & ORCH	C169
The Darktown Strutters' Ball*	HARRY ROY & ORCH	(164 165) C174
The Day You Came Along*	BBC DANCE ORCH (HENRY HALL)	211
	LEW STONE & BAND	(178) 229
The Echo Of A Song (comp Konig, Mann, Edgar)	ROY FOX & BAND	200
The Flat Foot Floogie*	FATS WALLER & CONTINENTAL RHYTHM	C149 C150
The Folks Who Live On The Hill*	STEPHANE GRAPPELLY & QUINTET	C173
The Free And Easy	AMBROSE & ORCH	(5 7) 195
The Fur Trappers' Ball	JOE LOSS & ORCH	219
The General's Fast Asleep*	JOE LOSS & ORCH	(105 C8) 216
The Gentleman Obviously Doesn't Believe In Love	LEW STONE & BAND	(185) 230

The Ghost Of Dinah	NAT GONELLA & GEORGIANS	208
The Girl With The Dreamy Eyes	LEW STONE & BAND	(185) 230
The Green Cockatoo	ROBERTO INGLEZ & ORCH	(94) C167
The Hut-Sut Song*	LEW STONE & BAND	(C105) C169
The Isle Of Innisfree	GERALDO STRINGS	204
The Lady Is A Tramp* (Carroll Re-Calls The Tunes No.1)	CARROLL GIBBONS (Piano solo)	207
The Lambeth Walk*	VICTOR SILVESTER & BALLROOM ORCH	227
The Language Of Love	LEW STONE & MONSEIGNEUR BAND	229
The Latin Quarter*	JOE LOSS & BAND	(105) 217
The Maharajah Of Magador	EDMUNDO ROS & RUMBA BAND	223
The Melody Maker* ("Bandwaggon" Film Selection)	JACK HYLTON & ORCH	212
The Mem'ry Of A Rose	ORGAN, THE DANCE BAND & ME	231
The Moment I Saw You (comp Gay, Clifford)	RAY NOBLE & ORCH	(124 137) C153
The Moochi	SPIKE HUGHES & DANCE ORCH	(74) C142
	JACK PAYNE & BBC DANCE ORCH	222
The Moon Got In My Eyes*	C.GIBBONS & SAVOY HOTEL ORPHEANS	(C19) C181
The Moon Is Low	JACK HARRIS & ORCH	C160
The Moon Was Yellow	BILLY COTTON & BAND	199
The Music Goes 'Round And Around*	BBC DANCE ORCH (HENRY HALL)	(66) C180
	NAT GONELLA & GEORGIANS	209
The Nearness Of You*	GERALDO & CONCERT ORCH	(53) 204
The New Swing Alphabet*	JACK JACKSON & ORCH	C174
The Night Is Young And You're So Beautiful	ROY FOX & ORCH	(41) 201
The Object Of My Affection*	HARRY ROY & ORCH	224
The Old Kitchen Kettle	J.HYLTON & OR/George Formby (C60)	C144 C170
The Old Man Of The Mountain*	RAY STARITA & AMBASSADORS	C174
The Old Spinning Wheel*	RAY NOBLE & ORCH	(125) C153
The One I Love Belongs To Somebody Else	VICTOR SILVESTER'S JIVE BAND	228
The Palais Glide (Medley), Part 1	JOE LOSS & BAND	218
The Peanut Vendor*	NAT GONELLA & GEORGIANS	208
The Penguin	AMBROSE & ORCH	(10) C160
There Goes That Song Again*	GERALDO & SAVOY HOTEL ORCH	202 C181
There I Go	ROYAL AIR FORCE DANCE ORCH	C169
There'll Come Another Day	ORGAN, THE DANCE BAND & ME	(187) 231
There's A Cabin In The Pines*	RAY NOBLE & ORCH	(126) 221
There's A New Day Comin'	HARRY ROY & ORCH	(157) C164
There's A New World*	JOE LOSS & ORCH	218
There's A Rickety Rackety Shack	THE KIT-CAT BAND	C178
There's A Ring Around The Moon*	JOE LOSS & BAND	(C103) 216
	BILLY MERRIN & COMMANDERS	C174
	R.NOBLE & NEW MAYFAIR DANCE O	(121 136) 220
There's A Small Hotel*	GERALDO & CONCERT ORCH	204
There's Honey On The Moon Tonight	VICTOR SILVESTER'S JIVE BAND	(C71) 228
There's No Green Grass Round The Old North Pole	CASANI CLUB ORCH	214
There's Nothing New To Tell You	LEW STONE & BAND	C169
There Was An Old Woman	CASANI CLUB ORCH	214
The Roy Rag	HARRY ROY & ORCH	(156 159) C164
The Scat Singers	HARRY ROY & ORCH	225
The Scene Changes	JOE LOSS & ORCH	(105 106) 217
These Foolish Things* (Carroll Re-Calls The Tunes No.3)	CARROLL GIBBONS (Piano solo)	207
The Sheik Of Araby*	HATCHETT'S SWINGTETTE	(70) C173
	NAT GONELLA & GEORGIANS	208
	NAT GONELLA (Tpt & Vcl) With Pno & Drs	210
(Silent Film Memories)	JOE LOSS & BAND	218
The Shrine Of Saint Cecilia	AMBROSE & ORCH	C169
The Skeleton In The Cupboard	NAT GONELLA & GEORGIANS	210
The Song Is You*	BBC DANCE ORCH (HENRY HALL)(C9 C141)	C157
The Sun Has Got His Hat On*	AMBROSE & ORCH	(C127) C154
The Teddy Bears' Picnic	BBC DANCE ORCH (H.HALL) (67 C24 C34)	C176

The Things We Did Last Summer	GERALDO & ORCH	202
The Thought Never Entered My Head	AMBROSE & ORCH	194
The Three Caballeros	EDMUNDO ROS & RUMBA BAND	223
The Toy Trumpet*	NAT GONELLA & GEORGIANS	210
The Very Thought Of You*	AMBROSE & ORCH	C160
	RAY NOBLE & ORCH	
	(129 131 135 139) 220 C153 C176	
The Waves Of The Ocean Are Whisp'ring Goodnight	BRAM MARTIN & BAND	(C133) C174
The Way You Look Tonight*	CARROLL GIBBONS (Piano solo)	207
The Wedding Samba*	EDMUNDO ROS & RUMBA BAND	223
The Whistler's Mother-In-Law	ROYAL AIR FORCE DANCE ORCH	C169
The Wind's In The West	ROY FOX & BAND	(35) C163
The Wishing Waltz	SQUADRONAIRES/Sam Browne	C146
The Words Are In My Heart	HARRY ROY & ORCH	224
They All Fall In Love	JACK HYLTON & ORCH	(C10) C179
They All Laughed	RONNIE MUNRO & ORCH With LARRY ADLER	C166
They Didn't Believe Me*	AMBROSE & ORCH	(7) C157
(Carroll Re-Calls The Tunes No.1)	CARROLL GIBBONS (Piano solo)	207
Things Are Looking Up (comp G. &. I. (Gershwin)	ROY FOX & ORCH	(41) 201
Things Are Looking Up (comp Grey,N.Gay)	JACK JACKSON & ORCH	213
Third Tiger Rag	See "Tiger Rag"	
This Is Romance*	RAY NOBLE & ORCH	(127 133) 221
This Is The Army, Mister Jones*	BILLY COTTON & BAND	C167
Three O'Clock In The Morning	STEPHANE GRAPPELLY & QUINTET	C173
Three Wishes*	LEW STONE & MONSEIGNEUR BAND	229
Tick-Tock Town	AMBROSE & ORCH	(12) 196
Tiger Rag* (Third)	BILLY COTTON & BAND	(25) 198
(MB1620-1)	JIMMY DORSEY Acc By SPIKE HUGHES & THREE BLIND MICE	(C46) C162
(MB1620-2)	JIMMY DORSEY Acc By SPIKE HUGHES & THREE BLIND MICE	C162
	STEPHANE GRAPPELLY & MUSICIANS	C173
	PHILIP LEWIS & ORCH	C148
	RONNIE MUNRO & ORCH With LARRY ADLER	C166
(Harry Roy Stage Show)	HARRY ROY & ORCH	225
Time On My Hands*	CARROLL GIBBONS (Piano solo)	207
	NEW MAYFAIR DANCE ORCH (R.NOBLE)	
	(118 131 135 C17 C93) C153	
Tina*	JOE LOSS & BAND	216
Ting-A-Ling (The Waltz Of The Bells)	HATCHETT'S SWINGTETTE	C173
Tip-Toe Through The Tulips* (Early Talkie Memories)	JOE LOSS & BAND	218
"Tip Top Tunes" Signature Tune	GERALDO & CONCERT ORCH	204
Tony's wife	CARROLL GIBBONS & BOY FRIENDS	(56) 206
Too Many Irons In The Fire*	ORGAN, THE DANCE BAND & ME	231
Too Many Tears	AMBROSE & ORCH	(7) 195
	BILLY COTTON & BAND	(22) C163
Too Romantic	LEW STONE & BAND	C169
Too Wonderful For Words	AMBROSE & ORCH	194
Tootin' Around	AMBROSE & ORCH	(10 C112) C160
Top Hat, White Tie And Tails*	AMBROSE & ORCH	196
	GERALDO & ORCH	204
Troublesome Trumpet*	HARRY ROY & ORCH	224 C164
Truckin'*	NAT GONELLA & GEORGIANS	208 210
Truckin' On Down*	HARRY ROY & ORCH	224
True	ROY FOX & BAND	200
Twelfth Street Rag*	HARRY ROY & ORCH	(156 159 160) C164
Twenty Million People	BBC DANCE ORCH (HENRY HALL)	211
Two Hearts On A Tree	BILLY COTTON & BAND	199
Two Sleepy People (Carroll Re-Calls The Tunes No.3)	CARROLL GIBBONS (Piano solo)	207
Two Trumpet Toot*	LEW STONE & BAND	(185) 230

Who Walks In When I Walk Out?	MADAME TUSSAUD'S DANCE ORCH	197
(take-1)	RAY NOBLE & ORCH	(128 C70) 221
(take-2)	RAY NOBLE & ORCH	(128 136) 220
Why Did I Kiss That Girl?*	SAVOY HAVANA BAND	C178
Why Do I Lie To Myself About You?	VICTOR SILVESTER'S JIVE BAND	227
Why Don't We Do This More Often?	LEW STONE & BAND	C175
Why Don't Women Like Me?	J.HYLTON & ORCH/Geo. Formby (C61)	C144 C170
Why Has A Cow Got Four Legs? ("Falling For You" Selection)	BILLY COTTON & BAND	198
Why Waste Your Tears?	LEW STONE & MONSEIGNEUR BAND	229
Wild Goose Chase	MADAME TUSSAUD'S DANCE ORCH	197
Will You Remember (Sweetheart?)*	GERALDO & ORCH	C174
Winter Wonderland*	AMBROSE & ORCH	196
Wishing*	CARROLL GIBBONS & SAVOY HOTEL ORPHEANS	206
Wish Me Luck (As You Wave Me Goodbye)*	ORGAN, THE DANCE BAND & ME	231
With My Eyes Wide Open I'm Dreaming	BBC DANCE ORCH (HENRY HALL)	211
Without A Song*	GERALDO & ORCH	C165
With Plenty Of Money And You*	JOE LOSS & BAND	218
With Thee I Swing	CARROLL GIBBONS & BOY FRIENDS	(56) 206
With The Wind And The Rain In Your Hair	ORGAN, THE DANCE BAND & ME	231
Ya Got Love	ROY FOX & BAND	(32) C174
Yeah Man (comp Sissle, Robinson)	NAT GONELLA & GEORGIANS	208
Yeah Man (comp Segure, Hardy, Schoen, Connor)*	JOE LOSS & ORCH	219
Yes Sir! That's My Baby*	HOTEL CECIL DANCE ORCH	222
Yes Suh!	LEW STONE & BAND	(185) 230
Yes Yes (My Baby Said Yes)*	AMBROSE & ORCH	(7 C20 C21) 195
Yira, Yira	GERALDO & GAUCH TANGO ORCH	C165
You Bought A New Kind Of Love To Me*	JACK HARRIS & ORCH	C160
You'd Be So Nice To Come Home To*	C.GIBBONS & SAVOY HOTEL ORPHEANS	(C10) C156
You Don't Understand ("Falling For You" Selection)	BILLY COTTON & BAND	198
You Gorgeous Dancing Doll*	GERALDO & SAVOY HOTEL ORCH	202
You Go To My Head*	JOE LOSS & BAND	218
You Gotta Know How To Dance*	HARRY ROY & ORCH	225
You Have Taken My Heart*	RAY NOBLE & ORCH	(128) 221
You Know What I'll Do	PHILIP BUCHEL With SPIKE HUGHES & THREE BLIND MICE	C162
You Leave Me Breathless	ROY FOX & ORCH	(41) 201
You'll Always Be Mine	GEORGE CHISHOLM & JIVE FIVE	(C72) C143
You Made Me Care*	JOE LOSS & ORCH	219
You Made Me Love You	HATCHETT'S SWINGTETTE	C173
You Must Have Been A Beautiful Baby*	JACK HYLTON & ORCH	212
You Oughta Be In Pictures*	ROY FOX & BAND	(36) 200
	RAY NOBLE & ORCH	(128 138) 221
You Rascal, You*	NAT GONELLA & GEORGIANS	209
(Medley)	HARRY ROY'S TIGER-RAGAMUFFINS	225
You're An Education*	JOE LOSS & BAND	218
You're Driving Me Crazy*	NOVELTY ORCH (R.NOBLE)	(118 138 C93) C153
	SQUADRONAIRES	168
You're Getting To Be A Habit With Me* ("42nd Street" Film Selection)	BILLY COTTON & BAND	198
You're Gonna Lose Your Gal	CARROLL GIBBONS & SAVOY HOTEL ORPHEANS	205
	MADAME TUSSAUD'S DANCE ORCH	197
You're Looking For Romance (I'm Looking For Love)	BRIAN LAWRENCE & LANSDOWNE ORCH	C174
You're Mine	OSCAR RABIN & BAND	C169
You're Mine, You	RAY NOBLE & ORCH	(125 133) 221
You're So Sweet To Remember	ORGAN, THE DANCE BAND & ME	231
You're Still In My Heart	MADAME TUSSAUD'S DANCE ORCH	197
You're Telling Me	ROY FOX & BAND	(33) C174
You're The Kind Of Baby For Me	SAVOY HOTEL ORPHEANS	205
You're The Top*	JACK HYLTON & ORCH	(C10) C156

You Started Something (comp. L.Robin, R.Rainger)*	ROYAL AIR FORCE DANCE ORCH	C169
You Took Advantage Of Me	VICTOR SILVESTER'S JIVE BAND	228
You Turned Your Head*	JACK JACKSON & ORCH	(C6) 213
You've Done Something To My Heart	GERALDO & SAVOY HOTEL ORCH	(C127) C181
You've Got Me Crying Again*	HARRY ROY & ORCH	224
You Went To My Head*	ROY FOX & ORCH	(41) 201
Zing! Went The Strings Of My Heart*	LEW STONE & BAND	(185 C20) 230

SECTION 4

INDEX OF VOCALISTS

The following Index covers albums listed in both the Catalogue and Supplement, and shows details of the bands with which a particular vocalist is featured and the albums in which recordings are contained.

Reference is made in the Index to the Album number shown in Column (1) of Section 1. The Index does not therefore show an Album number in instances where a particular track has been duplicated in another album, since in such cases details of the album containing the duplicate track are shown in Column (5) of Section 1. For example, the entry for Lou Abelardo shows that recordings made with Ambrose are to be found in Album 1, and by referring to that album it will be seen that the singer is featured on 13 tracks, one of which ("Painting The Clouds With Sunshine") is also contained in Collections C22, as shown in Column (5) but which is not referred to in the Index.

In accordance with practice used throughout the Supplement, the reference numbers of albums contained in the Catalogue are shown in parenthesis to distinguish them from those included in the Supplement.

Lou ABELARDO
With AMBROSE: (1 2) 194 C163
VAN PHILLIPS: (151)
RAY STARITA: (175)

Don ADAMS
With BILLY THORBURN (ODB&M): (187 C38)

Jill ALLEN
With SID PHILLIPS: (150)

Les ALLEN
With ALFREDO: (C135)
DURIUM DANCE BAND: (177)
FERRACHINI (L.FILLIS): (C91)
C.GIBBONS (SHO): (55 C14) 205 C163
HENRY HALL (BBCDO): (64-68 C4 C6 C9 C10 C16 C30) 211 C154 C157 C163
HARRY HUDSON: (C75)
CHARLIE KUNZ: 214
SYDNEY LIPTON: (103)
JACK PAYNE: (148)
HAL SWAIN: (C13 C28)

Rose ALPER
With JOE LOSS: (105)

Dorothy ALT
With LEW STONE: (178 183)
JAY WILBUR: (191)

Bob ARDEN
With AMBROSE: (C107)

Phil ARNOLD
With AMBROSE: (1 2)

Gerald ARTHUR
With HERMAN DAREWSKI: (C33)

Robert ASHLEY
With LOUIS LEVY & GBS: (C19)

Fred AUSTIN
With DEBROY SOMERS: C154

Max BACON
With AMBROSE: (8 12 C67)

George BARCLAY
With CHARLIE KUNZ: (98 99 C22)
MANTOVANI: (109)
FELIX MENDELSSOHN: (112-115)
BILLY THORBURN'S MUSIC: (C33)
BILLY THORBURN (ODB&M): (187) 231

Don Marino BARRETO
With OWN ORCH: (C38)

Tom BARRETT
With DEBROY SOMERS: (C51)

Don BARRIGO
With LEW STONE (part trio): (181 185) 230

Carl BARRITEAU
With HATCHETT'S SWINGTETTE: (70)
LEW STONE: (C105) C169

Elizabeth BATEY
With JOE LOSS: (C40) 219 C167?

Ken BEAUMONT
With ORLANDO: (C14)
BILLY TERNENT: (186)

Eve BECKE
With GERALDO: (49 51 52 53) 202
JACK HYLTON: (89 92 C10) C156
CHARLIE KUNZ: (98) 214
LOUIS LEVY: (101) C181
RAY NOBLE: (127 139 141)
OSCAR RABIN: (C132)

Harry BENTLEY
With C.GIBBONS (SHO): (C12 C20 C57) 205
JACK HARRIS: C160
CHARLIE KUNZ: (98) 214
SYDNEY LIPTON: (104)
ARTHUR ROSEBERY: (155?)
MADAME TUSSAUD'S D.O: 197
MAURICE WINNICK: C174

Eva BENYON
With BILLY TERNENT: (186)

Len BERMON
With HENRY HALL (BBCDO): (66 68)

Clem BERNARD
With BILLY COTTON (part trio): (26)

Peter BERNARD
With ALFREDO: (C1)

Gino BERNI
With GERALDO (GTO): (46 49)

Anita BEST
With BILLY TERNENT: (186)

Billy BISSETT
With OWN ORCH: (C32)

Betty BOLTON
With ROY FOX: (32)
RAY STARTIA: (175 C29)

Webster BOOTH
With FRED HARTLEY: (C64)

Connie BOSWELL
With AMBROSE: (C123)

Eve BOSWELL
With GERALDO: (53) 202 203

Suzanne BOTTERILL
With LEW STONE: (178)

Al BOWLLY
With EDGAR ADELER: (C91)
BROOKLYN BCSTRS (L.FILLIS): (C89)
BILLY COTTON: (C92)
DURIUM DANCE BAND: (176 177)
FRED ELIZALDE: (30 C80 C89) C163
FERRACHINI (L.FILLIS): (C91)
ROY FOX: (32-34 36 37 39 C82 C87 C88 C90 C91 C102 C133) C160 C163 C174
GERALDO: (49-52 C33 C138) 202
C.GIBBONS (SHO): (54 55 C57 C91 C117) 205 C153
HOWARD GODFREY: (C82 C83 C90 C133)
HARRY HUDSON: (C75 C82)
JACK JACKSON: (95)
KEN JOHNSON: (C84)

Al BOWLLY (Continued)
With ARTHUR LALLY: (C83 C98)
JACK LEON: (C90)
SYDNEY LIPTON: (104)
MONIA LITER: (C138)
JOCK MCDERMOTT: (C87)
PERCIVAL MACKEY: (C86)
MANTOVANI: (109)
BRAM MARTIN: (C133) C174
EARL MELVILLE (L.FILLIS): (C86)
FELIX MENDELSSOHN: (C133)
NEW MAYFAIR OR (R.MUNRO): (C10)
RAY NOBLE/NMDO: (118-140 142 143) 220 221 C153 C154 C156
SID PHILLIPS: (C82 C98)
VAN PHILLIPS: (151)
OSCAR RABIN: (153)
ORCHESTRA RAYMONDE: (C92)
DEBROY SOMERS: (C117)
LEW STONE: (178-184 C83 C87 C88 C98 C133) 229 C157 C174 C179
JAY WILBUR: (C86)
JAY WILBUR: (ALDW PLYRS): (C86)
REGINALD WILLIAMS: (C33)
MAURICE WINNICK: (192 193 C132 C133)
MARIUS B. WINTER: (C80 C87 C89)

Ted BRANDT
With JACK HARRIS: (C1)

Alan BREEZE
With BILLY COTTON: (22-26 C3 C8 C11 C12 C14 C23 C32 C51 C63 C105 C115 C130 C140) 198 199 C146 C167

Eddie BRIANT
With SYDNEY LIPTON: (C36)

Elizabeth BROOKE (Princess Pearl)
With HARRY ROY: (C27)

Sam BROWNE
With AMBROSE: (2-15 C3 C6 C9 C11 C14 C15 C24 C29 C51 C80 C102 C103 C127 C130 C139) 194-196 C148 C154 C157 C159 C160 C163 C179
BERTINI: (C80)
BLUE LYRES: (C3 C6 C30 C139)
BLUE MOUNTAINEERS: (C100 C102) C160
BILLY COTTON: (22 23 25) 198 199 C163)
HENRY HALL (BBCDO): 211
JACK HARRIS: (69 C8 C51)
JACK HYLTON: (76-78 80 82-86 92 93 C4 C5 C10-C13 C15) 212 C156
HARRY LEADER: (C36)
LOUIS LEVY: (101)
SYDNEY LIPTON: (103 C24)
JOE LOSS: (C37)
MANTOVANI: (110)
BILLY MERRIN: C20
RAY NOBLE: (141)
VAN PHILLIPS: (151)
BILLY REID & LPAB: (C126)
PRIMO SCALA'S ACC BD: (17)

Sam BROWNE (Continued)
With GEO SCOTT-WOOD (LPAB): (168 C35)
GEO SCOTT-WOOD (SIX SWINGERS): (166 C8 C16 C35)
SQUADRONAIRES: C146 C172
RAY STARITA: (175 C63) C174
LEW STONE: (178 182 183 185 C17 C140) C169 C176
BILLY TERNENT: (C10 C32)
JAY WILBUR: (191 C105 C107)
JAY WILBUR: (RHYTHM RASCS): (C131)

George BUCK
With CHARLIE KUNZ: 214

Sid BUCKMAN
With BILLY COTTON: (21 22)
ROY FOX: (33 35 36 39-41 43 44 C8 C90) 200 C174
JACK HYLTON: (C127) 212
BILLY TERNENT: (186)

Betty BUCKNELLE
With HENRY HALL (BBCDO): (66?)

Bob BUSBY
With JACK PAYNE (BBCDO) (part trio): (146 C29) 222 C154

Len CAMBER
With GERALDO: (50 52 53 C10) 202 203 C156

Billie CAMPBELL
With C.GIBBONS(SHO): (58 C18)
HATCHETT'S SWINGTETTE: (70 C140) C173

Jimmy CAMPBELL
With LOUIS LEVY: (C31)

Eddie CANTOR
With AMBROSE: (C123)

Les CAREW
With AMBROSE: (C107 C140)

Dorothy CARLESS
With AMBROSE: (14) C169
GERALDO: (49 50 52 53 C9 C10 C37 C99 C141) 202 203 C156
HATCHETT'S SWINGTETTE: (70 C107) C172 C174
RAY NOBLE: (C19)?
RAF DANCE ORCH: (C104) C169
JAY WILBUR: (C105) C175
(See also CAVENDISH THREE)

Elsie CARLISLE
With AMBROSE: (7 9 11-13 C20 C80 C102 C103) 195 C159 C174
JACK HARRIS: (69 C24)

Una Mae CARLISLE
With OWN BAND: (C46)

CARLYLE COUSINS (Cecile Petrie, Pauline Lister & Lillian Taylor)
With AMBROSE: (3 6 7) 195 C157
LEN FILLIS: (C98)
C.GIBBONS (SHO): (55 C117) 205

CARLYLE COUSINS (Continued)
With CHARLIE KUNZ: (99) 214

Paul CARPENTER
With C.GIBBONS (SHO): (58 C41 C57)
TED HEATH: (72)

Carole CARR
With GERALDO: (53 C51) 202 204

Rita CARR
With LEW STONE: C169

CAVENDISH THREE (Kay Cavendish, Pat Rignold & Dorothy Carless)
With JAY WILBUR: (191 C115)

Sylvia CECIL
With JACK HARRIS: (C16)
JAY WILBUR: (191)

Mary CHARLES
With LEW STONE: (181)

Harold "Chips" CHIPPENDALL
With BILLY COTTON: (24 25) 199
SYDNEY LIPTON: (104 C80 C138) C174

Wendy CLAIRE
With LEW STONE: C169

Diana CLARE (Esther COLEMAN)
With HARRY ROY: (C10) C156

Helen CLARE
With BILLY THORBURN (ODB&M): (187 C39) 231

Norma CLARKE
With JACK WHITE: (C35)

Archie COATES
With FELIX MENDELSSOHN: (112 114)

Peggy COCHRANE
With JACK JACKSON: 213

Esther COLEMAN
With CARROLL GIBBONS (SHO): 205
(See also Diana Clare)

Sid COLIN
With GERALDO: 202
RAF DANCE ORCH: (173 174 C80 C104 C105) C169
LEW STONE: (178 181 C80 C132)

Eddie COLLIS
With KIT-CAT BAND: (C137) C178
RONNIE MUNRO: (C135)
NEW MAYFAIR D.O.(C.GIBBONS): (C121) C163
PICCADILLY PLAYERS: (C29 C58)
SYD ROY: C164
RAY STARITA: (175 C5 C13)

Bobbie COMBER
With RAY NOBLE: (C127)

Jack COOPER
With AMBROSE: (9-12 14 15 C102 C103 C107 C140) 196 C160 C169
JACK HARRIS: (69)

Jack COOPER (Continued)
With JACK JACKSON: (C80) C174
JACK HYLTON: (C8)
RONNIE MUNRO: (C6 C127) C180
PRIMO SCALA: (17 18)
JAY WILBUR: (C105)

Mae COOPER
With CARL BARRITEAU: (C105 C125)

Sam COSTA
With BERT FIRMAN: (C32)
JACK HYLTON: (86 92 93)
JACK JACKSON: 213
JOE LOSS: 218
LOU PREAGER: (C80)
PRIMO SCALA: (17 18)
GEO SCOTT-WOOD (LPAB): (168 C126)
GEO SCOTT-WOOD (6 SWINGERS): (167)
DEBROY SOMERS: (C8)
MAXWELL STEWART: (C132)
LEW STONE: (178 181 C132)
SWINGTIMERS: (C77)
JAY WILBUR: (191 C115 C132)
JAY WILBUR (RHYTHM RASCS): (C131)
MAURICE WINNICK: (192 193 C3 C24 C31 C80)

Ken CROSSLEY
With MANTOVANI: (109)
BILLY MERRIN: (C80 C102)

Joe CROSSMAN
With AMBROSE: (7 8)
BLUE LYRES: (C20)
HARRY ROY: (C78)
LEW STONE: (178 179 181-183 185 C17 C104) 230

Gene CROWLEY
With BRAM MARTIN: (C24 C32)

The CUBS (Les Lambert, Ivor Mairants and Harry Gold)
With ROY FOX: (33 35-37 40 41) 201 C163 C174

Bill CURRIE
With HARRY ROY: (156-163 C3 C4 C9 C10 C14 C16-C19 C23 C27 C36 C130) 224 225 C156

Betty DALE
With JOE LOSS: (105) 217

Bob DALE
With GERALDO: 204
OSCAR RABIN: (153 C104 C105) C169

Evelyn DALL
With AMBROSE: (9 12 14 15 C106 C119 C132) C160 C169

Chappie D'AMATO
With J.HYLTON (part trio): (76-78 80-82 85 90 C2 C5 C7 C10 C15) C156 C179
JACK JACKSON (part trio): (95 C6 C20) 213

Joe DANIELS
With HOT SHOTS: (27)

Louis DAVIDS
With AMBROSE: (C52)

Beryl DAVIES
With No.1 BALLOON CENTRE D.O. (P.FENOULHET): (31 C40)
GERALDO: (49 50)
STEPHANE GRAPPELLY: C173
HATCHETT'S SWINGTETTE: (70) C173
OSCAR RABIN: (153 C104 C105 C132) C169 C174
RAF DANCE ORCH: (174 C104)

Ivor DAVIES
With EDDIE CARROLL: (C33)
SYDNEY LIPTON: (C35)
BILLY REID & ACC BD: (C126)

Dawn DAVIS
WIth CHARLIE KUNZ: 214
RAY NOBLE: (127)

Julie DAWN
With CARROLL GIBBONS (SHO): (C41)
HARRY LEADER: (C37)
LOU PREAGER: (152)
HARRY ROY: (C36)
BILLY THORBURN (ODB&M): 231
LEON VAN STRATEN: (C33)
ERIC WINSTONE (ACC BD): (C38 C130)
ERIC WINSTONE (SW QRT): (C18 C37)

Frances DAY
With RAY NOBLE: (125)

Alan DEAN
With AMBROSE: (C115)
CARROLL GIBBONS: (58)
OSCAR RABIN: (C104)

Frances DEE
With BILLY TERNENT: (186)

Peggy DELL
With ROY FOX: (35 36 39) 200 C163
JACK HYLTON: (90-92) 212

Johnny DENIS
With NOVELTY SWINGTETTE: C172

Denny DENNIS
With AMBROSE: (10 14 15 C67 C103) C169
P.FENOULHET & SKYROCKETS: (C99)
ROY FOX: (35-41 43 44 C9 C17 C22 C23 C32 C64 C138 C141) 200 201
JACK HYLTON: (90) 212
JACK JACKSON: (95)

Terry DEVON
With CARROLL GIBBONS: (58)
OSCAR RABIN: C169
B.THORBURN (ODB&M): (187 C33) 231

Hughie DIAMOND
With JACK HARRIS: (69)
RONNIE MUNRO:(C8)

Hughie DIAMOND (Continued)
With LEW STONE: (C132)
MAURICE WINNICK: (193)

DIANE (Dorothy WICK)
With OSCAR RABIN: (153 C105 C107) C169

Dan DONOVAN
With HIS MUSIC: (C32)
HENRY HALL (BBCDO): (66-68 C3 C10 C12 C18 C19 C23 C47 C127) 211 C156
DEBROY SOMERS: (172 C2 C12 C18 C30)
MADAME TUSSAUD'S D.O: 197
JAY WILBUR: (191)

Nadia DORE
With GERALDO: (53)

Nadia DORE'S DEBONAIRES
With FELIX MENDELSSOHN: (114 115)

Paul DORN
With JACK HYLTON: (80)

Fred DOUGLAS
With DURIUM DANCE BAND: (C134)
PERCIVAL MACKEY: (108 C135 C137)

Leslie DOUGLAS
With AMBROSE: C169 C172
NO.1 BALLOON CENTRE D.O. (P. FENOULHET): (31)
C.GIBBONS (SHO): (58 C10 C38 C40 C57)
HENRY HALL: (68 C8 C16 C33)
SKYROCKETS DANCE BAND (P. FENOULHET): (C107)

Sally DOUGLAS
With GERALDO: (53 C9 C41) 203

Jack DOYLE
With BILLY COTTON: (26) C161?

Johnny EAGER
With SID PHILLIPS: (150)

Michael EASTLEY
With GERALDO: (C8)

Jim EASTON
With LEW STONE (178 182)

Rex EATON
With AMBROSE: (C140)

EDDIE & REX (Brian Lawrence & Jack Lorimer)
With RAY NOBLE: (141)

Roy EDWARDS
With GERALDO: 204
FELIX MENDELSSOHN: (114)

Austin EGEN
With JACK HYLTON: (81)

Ray ELLINGTON
With HARRY ROY: (161 162)

George ELRICK
With SWING MUSIC MAKERS: (C32)
HENRY HALL (BBCDO): (66-68 C12) C180

Dolly ELSIE
With BILLY COTTON: (26 C105)
JACK HYLTON: (90 92 93) 212

Maurice ELWIN
With ARCADIANS D.O (B.FIRMAN): (C15 C55 C94) C148
DEVONSHIRE REST D.O (B.FIRMAN): (C15)
BERT FIRMAN'S D.O: (C53)
JOHN FIRMAN: (C30)
C.GIBBONS (SHO) : (C57) 205
PHILIP LEWIS: C148
PERCIVAL MACKEY: (108)
ORPHEANS DANCE BD (B.FIRMAN): (C15)
VAN PHILLIPS: (151)
RHYTHMIC EIGHT (B.FIRMAN): (C15 C24 C53 C55 C75 C94) C148
RAY STARITA: (175)
WEST END PLAYERS (J. HARRIS): (C9)

Paul ENGLAND
With JACK HYLTON: (C9)

Clive ERARD
With JACK HYLTON: (90)

George EVANS
With FOUR STARS: (C77)
GERALDO: (50 C35 C37 C99) 202 203
SQUADRONAIRES: (174 C104)

Jean FARRAR
With HARRY ROY: (158)

Sonny FARRAR
With JACK HYLTON (part trio): (87-89) C163

Bobby FARRELL
With SYD SEYMOUR: (C32)

Harry FAY
With BILLY COTTON: (C127)

Jewel FAYE
With JACK HYLTON; (90 93)

Joe FERRIE
With ROY FOX: (C90 C103)
GEORGE SCOTT-WOOD: (C16)
LEW STONE: (178 183-185 C17 C31 C103) 230

Gerry FITZGERALD
With SYDNEY KYTE: (C80)
LOUIS LEVY: (101)
SYDNEY LIPTON: (104)
DEBROY SOMERS: (C19)

Bud FLANAGAN & Chesney ALLEN
With HENRY HALL (BBCDO): (64 66) 211

George FORMBY
With JACK HYLTON: (C60 C61) C144 C145 C170

Teddy FOSTER
With BILLY COTTON: (24 25 C3) 198

FOUR MUSKETEERS
With HENRY HALL (BBCDO): (65 C9)

Derek FRANCIS
With GERALDO: (53) 204

Dave FULLERTON
With STEPHANE GRAPPELLY: C173

Ronnie GENARDER
With ROY FOX: (35)
JACK PAYNE: (C132)

GEORGINA (Thelma JAGGER)
With IVY BENSON: (C40)
GERALDO: (C39)

GERALDETTES
With GERALDO: (48)

GERALDTONES
With GERALDO: (53) 203

Carroll GIBBONS
With HIS SHO: (55 56 C9 C37 C39 C57 C127) 206
OWN PIANO ACC: (56) 206 207

Burton GILLIS
With HENRY HALL (BBCDO): (67 68)

Bruts GONELLA
With BILLY COTTON: (22) 198
NAT GONELLA: (62)

Nat GONELLA
With STANLEY BLACK: C160
BLUE MOUNTAINEERS: (C100) C160
BILLY COTTON: (21 24)
ROY FOX: (32 34 37 C87 C90 C103)
HIS GEORGIANS: (60-63 C4 C8 C10 C14 C27 C32 C36 C37 C49 C51 C70 C100 C104) 208-210 C167 C172
INSTRUMENTAL ACC: (59) C142
SYDNEY LIPTON: (103)
RAY STARITA: (C102)
LEW STONE: (178 179 182 184 185 C17 C100 C103) 230

Niela GOODELLE
With HENRY HALL: (C16)

Lola GORDON
With DURIUM DANCE BAND: (C134)

Gary GOWAN
With OSCAR RABIN: (153) C169

Cyril GRANTHAM
With BILLY COTTON: (21-23) 198 C163
GERALDO: (48 49 51-53 C9 C14 C25 C35 C64 C97 C99 C132 C138) 202 C174
SYDNEY LIPTON: (104)
JOE LOSS: 219
PRIMO SCALA (17 18 C118)
JAY WILBUR: (191)

Barry GRAY
With ROY FOX: (40 41 C17) 201

Peter GRAY
With LEW STONE: (C104)

Johnny GREEN
With GERALDO: (49 50 C10 C41) 202 C156 C167
HARRY ROY: (162) C167

Paula GREEN
With JOE LOSS: (C16 C36) 219

GREENE SISTERS
With SID PHILLIPS: C174
JAY WILBUR: (191)

Eddie GROSSBART
With AMBROSE: 194
NEW MAYFAIR D.O (C.GIBBONS): (C121)
PICCADILLY PLAYERS: (C7 C29 C58) C148
RAY STARITA: (175) C163

HAMILTON SISTERS & FORDYCE
With SAVOY ORPHEANS: (C7) C158

Tommy HANDLEY
With JACK HYLTON: (91)

Kay HARDING
With DON MARINO BARRETO: (C38)
HARRY ROY: (163)
BILLY THORBURN (ODB&M): 231

Doris HARE
With SYDNEY LIPTON: (103)

HARMONY THREE
With GEORGE SCOTT-WOOD: (C16)

Nat HARRIS
With MADAME TUSSAUD'S D.O.: 197

Bob HARVEY
With GERALDO: (53)

HAWAIIAN SISTERS
With FELIX MENDELSSOHN: (114 115)

Johnny HELFER
With RHYTHMIC EIGHT (B.FIRMAN): (C55)

Chick HENDERSON
With JOE LOSS: (105-107 C3 C14 C16 C35 C47 C63 C127) 216-219
GEORGE SCOTT-WOOD (LPAB): (168)
BILLY THORBURN (ODB&M): (187) 231

HENDERSON TWINS
With KEN JOHNSON: (C84)

Leonard HENRY
With RAY NOBLE: (121)

HERON SISTERS
With BRAM MARTIN: (C32)

Ronnie HILL
With JACK HYLTON: (93)
CHARLIE KUNZ: (98)
RINALDO'S ACCORDIONS: (C80)
PRIMO SCALA: (17 C22)

Al HOFFMAN
With LEW STONE: (185 C9 C17) 230

Leslie HOLMES
With JACK PAYNE: (147) C154

Joy HOODLESS
With GERALDO: 204

Ruth HOWARD
With BILLY TERNENT: (186)

Harry HUDSON
With HIS MELODY MEN: (C1)

Alberta HUNTER
With JACK JACKSON: (95 96) 213

Jackie HUNTER
With GERALDO: (C36) 203

Rusty HURREN

With LOU PREAGER: (152)

Leslie HUTCHINSON (Hutch)
With HARRY ROY: (C110 C124) C164

Pat HUTTON
With ROBERTO INGLEZ: (94)

Pat HYDE
With NAT GONELLA: (62)

Jack HYLTON
With OWN ORCH: (75-78 83 88 89 C2 C7 C9 C10 C11 C15 C137) C156 C158

Roberto INGLEZ
With OWN ORCH: (94)

THE JACKDAWS
With GEORGE SCOTT-WOOD (6 SWINGERS): (C14)
LEW STONE: (180 183 C88)

Ellis JACKSON
With BILLY COTTON: (22 24 25)

Jack JACKSON
With OWN ORCH: (95 96 C6 C19 C20 C24 C80) 213 C174
JACK HYLTON (part trio): (76 78 80 84 C5 C7)
RAY NOBLE: (118)
JACK PAYNE: (147)

Dick JAMES
With PAUL FENOULHET: (31)
GERALDO: (53 C9) 204

Don JOHNSON
With KEN JOHNSON: (C35)

Gwen JONES
With GERALDO: (C127) C181

Trevor JONES
With GERALDO: (C12)

Bobby JOY
With ROY FOX: (41 C104)

JUNE
With HENRY HALL (BBCDO): (67)

Ada KAHN
With NEW MAYFAIR D.O.(C.GIBBONS):(C9)

Alan KANE
With AMBROSE: (C107)
JOE LOSS: (C38)
MANTOVANI: (110 C140)
NEW MAYFAIR D.O: (C37)
GEORGE SCOTT-WOOD (LPAB): (168)
LEW STONE: (183-185 C9 C11 C19 C20) 230
B.THORBURN (ODB&M): (187 C36 C37) 231
ERIC WINSTONE: (C9 C39 C40)

Edna KAYE
With C.GIBBONS (SHO): (C10 C18) C156
LOU PREAGER: (C41 C99)

Harry KAYE
With JOE LOSS: (C9 C39 C40 C41)
BILLY THORBURN (ODB&M): 231

Annette KEITH
with MADAME TUSSAUD'S D.O: 197

Betty KENT
With JACK SIMPSON: (C107)

Frank KERSLAKE
With GEORGE SCOTT-WOOD (6 SWINGERS):(167)

THE KEYNOTES
With HARRY ROY: (164 165) C174
PRIMO SCALA: (17 19) C171 C172

David KIDD
With JACK HYLTON: (C102)

Irene KING
With BILLY TERNENT: (186)

Marjorie KINGSLEY
With HATCHETT'S SWINGTETTE: (70)
HARRY ROY: (158 163 C37 C38 C40)

Stanley KIRKBY
With JACK PAYNE: (148)

Pat KIRKWOOD
With JACK HYLTON: (C10) C156

Arthur LALLY
With RHYTHMIC EIGHT (B.FIRMAN): (C55)

Lupino LANE
With HENRY HALL (BBCDO): (67)

Fred LATHAM
With JACK HARRIS: (C4)
JACK JACKSON: (95 C5 C6 C12 C20 C23) 213

Brian LAWRENCE
With HIS SEXTET: (C22)
HIS LANS HSE SEXT: (C103 C132)
HIS LANS ORCH: (C80 C103) C174
QUAGLINO QUARTET: (C103)
HIS ORCH: (C115)
LOUIS DE VRIES: C160
C.GIBBONS (SHO): (C3 C4 C9 C23 C31 C57)
FRED HARTLEY: (C81)

Brian LAWRENCE (Continued)
With JACK HYLTON: (93) 212
NEW MAYFAIR D.O (C.GIBBONS): C25)
NEW MAYFAIR D.O (P.MACKEY): (C18)
GEO SCOTT-WOOD (6 SWINGERS): (167)
LEW STONE: (178 C132)
(See also EDDIE & REX)

Barry LEARY
With AL COLLINS: C174

Benny LEE
With STANLEY BLACK: (C107)
JOHNNY CLAES: (C38 C71)
P. FENOULHET (NO.1
BALLOON CENTRE D.O): (C41)
HARRY PARRY (RRCS): (144)
OSCAR RABIN: C169
LEW STONE: (C104 C105) C175

Buddy LEE
With BILLY MAYERL: (C114)

Eddie LEE
With JOE DANIELS: (28 C36)

Mary LEE
With ROY FOX: (36 39-41 43 44 C17 C19
C33 C138) 201

Len LEES
With ARTHUR ROSEBERY: (155 C4 C29)

Anne LENNER
with C.GIBBONS (BOY FRDS): (57)
C.GIBBONS (SHO): (56 58 C3 C9 C10
C11 C16 C19 C24 C35
C36 C51 C57)
206 C156 C181
LOUIS LEVY: (101)
JOE LOSS: (105)
FRANK WEIR (ASTOR CLUB 7): (C105)
JAY WILBUR: (191 C105)
MAURICE WINNICK: (192)

Shirley LENNER
With JOE LOSS: 218

Queenie LEONARD
With PERCIVAL MACKEY: (C29)

Archie LEWIS
With GERALDO: (C101) 203 204

Kealoha LIFE
With FELIX MENDELSSOHN: (115)

Janet LIND
With LOUIS LEVY: (101)

Celia LIPTON
With JACK HYLTON: 212
SYDNEY LIPTON: (C35)
LEW STONE: (183)

Renee LISTER
With HARRY ROY: (163 C38)

Ella LOGAN
With AMBROSE: (5-8 C14 C29)
ROY FOX: (C90)
JACK HYLTON: (C6)

Eve LOMBARD
With HARRY ROY: (164 165)

Santiago LOPEZ
With EDMUNDO ROS: (C38)

Jack LORIMER
See EDDIE & REX

Doreen LUNDY
With PAUL FENOULHET: (31)

Vera LYNN
With AMBROSE: (14 15 C67 C103)
CHARLIE KUNZ: (98 99) C174
ORLANDO: (C26)
RHYTHM RASC. (J.WILBUR): (C67)
PRIMO SCALA (H.BIDGOOD): (C67)
MAURICE WINNICK: (193)

Rosa MACARI
With FELIX MENDELSSOHN: (112 114)

Lydia MACDONALD
With TED HEATH: (72)

Helen MACK
With NAT GONELLA: (C104) C167
LEW STONE (NOVA-TONES):
(C104) C174

Helen MACKAY
With LEW STONE: (178)

Bob MALLIN
With HENRY HALL: (68 C8)

June MALO
With JACK HYLTON: (90 92)

Alice MANN
With BILLY BISSETT: (C32)
FREDDY GARDNER: (45)
JACK HYLTON: (80 92 93)

Bob MANNING
With JACK PAYNE (part trio): (146
C24 C29) 222 C154

Rita MARLOWE
With STANLEY BLACK: (C107)
ERIC WINSTONE: (C9)

Glen MARTIN
With RAOC BLUE ROCKETS: (C16 C38)

Kitty MASTERS
With HENRY HALL (BBCDO): (66)

Dick MAXWELL
With FRED ELIZALDE: (30)

Ronaldo MAZAR
With EDMUNDO ROS: 223

Florine McKINNEY
With JACK JACKSON: (C12)

George MELACHRINO
With AMBROSE: C169
C.GIBBONS (SHO): (58 C3 C9 C10 C57)
206 C155 C156

Mabel MERCER
With HARRY ROY: (C27)

Al MERRALL
With MANTOVANI: (110)

Billy MERRIN
With HIS COMMANDERS: (C24) C174

Jimmy MESSINI
With GEORGE GLOVER: (C102)
NAT GONELLA: (63) 208
TEDDY JOYCE: (C102) C174
JOE LOSS: (105 C102 C103 C115) 216 217 C174
BILLY THORBURN (ODB&M): (187)
MAURICE WINNICK: C174

Ray MILLAR
With MANTOVANI: (110)

Dinah MILLER
With JACK HARRIS: (69 C24 C33)
OSCAR RABIN: (C32)
HARRY ROY: 225

Jimmy MILLER
With RAF DANCE ORCH: (173 174 C48 C105 C107 C125) C169
SQUADRONAIRES: (174 C104 C125) C146

Annette MILLS
With JOE LOSS: (105) 217

Billy MILTON
With NEW MAYFAIR D.O (C.GIBBONS):(C121)
VAN PHILLIPS: (151)
RUDY STARITA: (C29)

Louisa MOE
With FELIX MENDELSSOHN: (112)

Pulu MOE
With FELIX MENDELSSOHN: (113)

Edward MOLLOY
With LOUIS LEVY: (101)

Molly MORELIE
With HENRY HALL: (68)

Ivor MORETON
With HARRY ROY: (157-159 161 C4 C6 C10 C11 C12 C18 C25 C27) 224 C156 C163 C164

Tony MORRIS
With JACK WHITE: (C14 C33 C35 C36)

Stella MOYA
With NAT GONELLA: (63 C32)

Billy MUNN
With JACK HYLTON: (87) C143

Anna NEAGLE
With GERALDO: (C12)

Max & Harry NESBITT
With JACK HYLTON: C154

Sydney NESBITT
With BERT FIRMAN: (C137)

Raymond NEWELL
With DEBROY SOMERS: (C130)

Billy NICHOLLS
With OSCAR RABIN: C174

Joy NICHOLS
With HARRY ROY: (164)

Alfie NOAKES
With LEW STONE: (178 181 185 C17 C24) 230

Kenny NOBLE
With PRIMO SCALA (H.BIDGOOD): C146

Ray NOBLE
With OWN ORCH: (124 141)

Cavan O'CONNOR
with GERALDO: (48)
LONDON PIANO ACC BAND: (168)
RAY NOBLE: (141)
PRIMO SCALA: (17 18)
TROISE: (C118)
MAURICE WINNICK: (192)

Ronnie O'DELL
With LEW STONE: (183 C104 C132) C146 C174)
MAURICE WINNICK: (192 193)

Jack O'HAGAN
With ROY FOX: (C104)

Barrie OLIVER
With PICCADILLY PLAYERS: (C58)

Pat O'MALLEY
With JACK HYLTON: (77 78 81-89 92 93 C2 C4 C6 C13 C14 C18 C29 C80 C102 C103 C122 C127) 212 C156
JACK HYLTON (part trio): (77 80-82 84 85 87-90) C163 C179
CHARLIE KUNZ: (98)
NEW MAYFAIR D.O.(R.NOBLE): (C121)
NIGHT CLUB KINGS (R.NOBLE): (C70) C148
PRIMO SCALA: (17)
JAY WILBUR: (C80)

Eileen ORCHARD
With LOU PREAGER: (152)

Pat O'REGAN
With PRIMO SCALA: (17 18)
JAY WILBUR: (191 C115)

Primrose ORROCK
With JACK HYLTON: (90 C8) 212
BILLY THORBURN (ODB&M): 231

THE OVALTINEYS
With GERALDO: C165

Rex OWEN
With ROY FOX: (39)

Vivien PAGET
With FRANK WEIR: C174

Barbara PALMER
With BILLY THORBURN (ODB&M): (187)

PARADISE ISLAND TRIO
With FELIX MENDELSSOHN: (112 114)

Jack PARNELL
With TED HEATH: (71 72)

Norman PATRICK
With GERALDO: (53)

Graham PAYN
With CARROLL GIBBONS (SHO): (C130)

Jack PAYNE
With HIS BBC D.O: (145 146 C24 C29 C127) 222 C154
HIS BAND: (147 148 C80)
HOTEL CECIL ORCH: (C137)

Bob & Alf PEARSON
With JACK PAYNE: (148)

Cecile PETRIE
With C.GIBBONS (BOY FRDS): (56) 206
C.GIBBONS (SHO): (C5)
JACK HYLTON: (87 89)
DEBROY SOMERS: (C25)
(See also CARLYLE COUSINS)

Phil PHILLIPS
With BILLY COTTON: (26)

Jack PLANT
With ROY FOX: (33 35 36 C80) C163
C.GIBBONS (SHO): (54-56) 205 206
JACK HYLTON: (83 85)
TEDDY JOYCE: (C31 C130)
SYDNEY LIPTON: (103 C3)
MANTOVANI: (110)
NEW MAYFAIR D.O (R.NOBLE): (C121) C163
NIGHT CLUB KINGS (R.NOBLE): (C70)
RAY NOBLE: (139-142)
JACK PAYNE (BBCDO): 222
JACK PAYNE (BAND): (148)
WILL PERRY: (C94)
VAN PHILLIPS: (151)
GEORGE SCOTT-WOOD: (C18)
ERIC WINSTONE SWING QRT: (C107)

Eddie POLA
With JACK HARRIS: (C1)

The QUADS
With SQUADRONAIRES: (174 C104 C107 C125) C146 C168

THE RADIO THREE
(Kay Cavendish, Joy Worth & Ann Carring)
With GERALDO: (C120) C165
PRIMO SCALA: (17)
LEW STONE: (185 C9) 230

Pamela RAINER
With BILLY THORBURN (ODB&M): (187)

Bert RALTON
With HAVANA BAND: (C137)

Cyril RAMON NEWTON
With SAVOY HAVANA BD: (C1 C7 C56) C178
SAVOY ORPHEANS: (C4 C7 C13 C28 C56 C135) C163
DEBROY SOMERS: (172)

Helen RAYMOND
With BILLY MERRIN: (C102)
BILLY THORBURN (ODB&M): 231
(See also THE RHYTHM SISTERS)

Monte REY
With GERALDO (GTO): (47 48 C79 C97 C119 C138) C165
GERALDO ORCH: (48 53 C118 C120) C165
JOE LOSS: (105 107 C33 C64 C79) 218 219

THE RHYTHM SISTERS
(Kay Munro-Smith, Jean Conibear and Helen Raymond)
With AMBROSE: (10 12 13 15) C160
JOE LOSS: (C103)
JAY WILBUR: (C80)

Paul RICH
With LOU PREAGER: (152 C41 C48 C99) C176)

Foster RICHARDSON
With JACK PAYNE: (148)

Anita RIDDELL
With HENRY HALL: (68)

Hugo RIGNOLD
With JACK HYLTON (part trio): (76)

Jessie ROBBINS
With HARRY LEADER: (C31)

Stella ROBERTA
With MONTOVANI: (109 110)

Bette ROBERTS
With JOE LOSS: (C127) 219

Stuart ROBERTSON
With JACK HYLTON: (85 C4)
RONNIE MUNRO: (C28)

Phyllis ROBINS
With AMBROSE: (7) 195
HENRY HALL (BBCDO): (65 68) 211
JACK HYLTON: (88 C103)
CHARLIE KUNZ: 214
ORLANDO: (C20)
MADAME TUSSAUD'S D.O: 197
JAY WILBUR: (191)

Abe ROMAINE
With HARRY ROY (part trio): 225

EDMUNDO ROS
With HIS RUMBA BAND: (154 C39) 223 C174

Arthur ROSEBERY
With HIS KIT-CAT BD (part trio); (155 C29)

Val ROSING
With HIS SWING STARS: (C26)
HENRY HALL (BBCDO): (64 66-68 C3) C176
SPIKE HUGHES: (74) C162
RAY NOBLE: (141)
JACK PAYNE (BBCDO): (145 146) 222
JAY WILBUR: (C122)

Derek ROY
With GERALDO: (53 C40)

Harry ROY
With HIS ORCH: (156-165 C3 C4 C9 C10 C14 C17 C18 C24 C27 C31 C38 C40 C47 C63 C64 C65 C66 C130) 224 225 C156 C163 C164 C174
TIGER-RAGAMUFFINS: 225

THE ROYALISTS
With HARRY ROY: (163 C38)

Leslie SARONY
With BARNSTORMERS: C174
BILLY COTTON: (C134)
HENRY HALL (BBCDO): (66)
JACK HYLTON: (76 77 82 83)
JACK PAYNE: (147)
BILLY TERNENT: (186) C172

Elizabeth SCOTT
With HENRY HALL (BBCDO): (66)

Billy SCOTT-COOMBER
With JACK PAYNE (BBCDO): (145 146 C20) 222
JACK PAYNE (BAND): (147 148 C119 C132 C140) 222 C146
PRIMO SCALA: (18)

George SCOTT-WOOD
With "SILLY SYMPHONIC" ORCH: (C16)
SIX SWINGERS: (C16)
LONDON PIANO ACC BAND: (168)

SCOTT & WELDON
With RONNIE MUNRO: (C135)

Bob SHACKLETON
With GERALDO: (53)

Cyril SHANE
With P.FENOULHET SKYROCKETS: (31 C130)
GERALDO: (C99) 203

Anne SHELTON
With AMBROSE: (9 14 16 C68 C104 C105 C107) 146 C169
JACK HYLTON: (93 C8)
HARRY ROY: (165)

Judy SHIRLEY
With MAURICE WINNICK: (192 193)

Ralph SILVESTER
With PRIMO SCALA: (17)

Sid SIMONE
With PRIMO SCALA: (17)

Dorothy SQUIRES
With BILLY REID (LPAB): (C126)

Al STARITA
With KIT-CAT BAND: (97 C13)

Ray STARITA
With HIS AMBASSADORS BAND: (175)
PICCADILLY REVELS BD: (C28 C58)

Rudy STARITA
With PICCADILLY REVELS BAND: (C58)

Marjorie STEDEFORD
With JACK JACKSON: (C25)
BRIAN LAWRENCE: (C132)
GEO SCOTT-WOOD (6 SWGRS): (166 167)

Clem STEVENS
With JOE LOSS: (105 106 C130) 217

Donald STEWART
With AMBROSE: (11 12)

LEW STONE
With HIS BAND: (178 185 C17) 230

Lee STREET
With RAOC BLUE ROCKETS: (C38)

Ann STUART
With GERALDO: (53)

SUE & HER BOY FRIENDS
With JAY WILBUR: (191)

THE SUNNYSIDERS
With LOU PREAGER: (152)

Hal SWAIN
With HIS NEW PRINCES TORONTO BD: (C28)

THE SWINGTETTE
(Frances Jewel, Dorothy McCarthy, Ben Lake & Gene Lanham)
With JACK HYLTON: (80 90 92 93 C11) 212

Eric TANN
With RAOC BLUE ROCKETS: (C38)

Pat TAYLOR
With GERALDO: (53) 202
JACK HARRIS: (69 C24)

Beryl TEMPLEMAN
with ROY FOX: (C104)

Billy TERNENT
With JACK HYLTON (part trio): (76-78 80 81 82 85 87-90 C2 C5 C7 C10 C15) C156 C163 C179

Phyllis THACKERY
With HARRY ROY: (C27)

John THORNE
With HARRY HUDSON: (C1)

THREE BOYS & A GIRL
With GERALDO: (49 53 C10 C99) C156

THREE GINX
(Ivor Robinson, Jack Joy & Eric Hanley)
With AMBROSE: (6 7 C24)

THREE GINX (Continued)
With SYDNEY KYTE: (100)
RAY NOBLE: (119 141 142)
PRIMO SCALA: (17)

THREE JAYS
With JAY WILBUR: (C105)

THREE SISTERS
With HENRY HALL (BBCDO): (67 68)

THE TOPHATTERS
With GERALDO: (48 C97 C120) 203

Bruce TRENT
With JACK HYLTON: (92 93 C3 C8 C11 C18) 212 C180

Ken TUCKER
With JACK HYLTON: (93)

Sophie TUCKER
With HARRY ROY: (C111)

Alma VAINE
With C.GIBBONS & PLAYMATES: (54)

VALAIDA
With BILLY MASON: (188) C147
GEO SCOTT-WOOD: (188 189) C147

Dickie VALENTINE
With TED HEATH: (71 72)

Denny VAUGHAN
With GERALDO: (53) 203
C.GIBBONS (SHO): (58) C167
EDMUNDO ROS: (154)
CYRIL STAPLETON: (C107)

W. VERNON
With RAY NOBLE: (141 C121)

Doreen VILLIERS
With AMBROSE: (C107)
GERALDO: (49 53) 202 203
HARRY PARRY (RRCS): (144)

Tom WAREING
With JACK HYLTON: (93 C23) 212

Elizabeth WELCH
With BENNY CARTER QUINTET: (20)

WESTERN BROTHERS
With BILLY COTTON: (24) 198

JAY WHIDDEN
With HIS NEW MIDNIGHT FOLLIES BD: (190)
HIS CARLTON HOTEL BAND: (C1)

Tommy WHITEFOOT
With HENRY HALL (GLENEAGLES HOTEL BAND): (C102) C174

Jack WHITING
With CARROLL GIBBONS (SHO): (C59)

Eric WHITLEY
With C.GIBBONS (SHO): (58 C35 C57)
TEDDY JOYCE: (C19)
HARRY ROY: (165)

Duncan WHYTE
With OWN ORCH: (C77)

Joe WILBUR
With SAVOY QUARTET: (C7)

Dave WILKINS
With TED HEATH: (72)

Freddy WILLIAMS
With H.HALL (BBCDO) (part trio): (67 68)

Neville WILLIAMS
With GERALDO: 204

Nora WILLIAMS
With GEO SCOTT-WOOD (6 SWINGERS): (166)

Rita WILLIAMS
With CARROLL GIBBONS (SHO): (C57)
LOU PREAGER: (152)
BILLY THORBURN (ODB&M): 231

Bertha WILLMOTT
With RONNIE MUNRO: (C64)

Wally WINDSOR
With BILLY THORBURN (ODB&M): (187)

Anona WINN
With AMBROSE: (7) 195
C.GIBBONS (SHO): (C117)
SYDNEY LIPTON: (103)
RAY NOBLE: (122 140)

Tiny WINTERS
With HIS BOGEY SEVEN: (C72)
LEW STONE: (178 181-185 C17 C88) 230

Marcel WITTRISCH
With JACK HYLTON: (81 85)

Monty WOOLF
With PERCIVAL MACKEY: (C137)

Peggy WOOD
With C.GIBBONS (SHO): (C9)

Sally WOOD
With SQUADRONAIRES: (174)

George WRIGHT
With BILLY MERRIN: (C102)

Bert YARLETT
With HENRY HALL (BBCDO): (C4)
JACK HYLTON: (93 C10) 212
LEW STONE: (C22)

ADDENDUM

The following albums have been issued since the Supplement was completed. Details relating to these albums are not included in the Index Of Tune Titles or the Index Of Vocalists. They will, however, be fully incorporated into any later Supplement.

JACK HYLTON AND HIS ORCHESTRA (1931 To 1933) - Song Of Happiness : Saville SVL 187

Song Of Happiness (Pat O'Malley & Billy Munn)	1 Dec 1931	Dec F2701	
I Apologise (Pat O'Malley)	17 Dec 1931	Dec F2756	
Mona Lisa (Pat O'Malley)	22 Dec 1931	Dec F2757	
A Faded Summer Love (Pat O'Malley)	22 Dec 1931	Dec F2767	
By The Sycamore Tree (Pat O'Malley)	8 Feb 1932	Dec F2845	
Now's The Time To Fall In Love (Leslie Sarony)	8 Feb 1932	Dec F2823	
Goopy Geer (Pat O'Malley)	9 Feb 1932	Dec F2878	
Who's Your Little Who-Zis? (Pat O'Malley)	3 Mar 1932	Dec F2904	
With Love In My Heart (Pat O'Malley)	3 Mar 1932	Dec F2904	
Rain On The Roof (Pat O'Malley)	20 Apr 1932	Dec F2939	
With All My Love And Kisses (Pat O'Malley)	20 Apr 1932	Dec F2938	
How Long Will It Last? (Pat O'Malley)	28 Apr 1932	Dec F2984	
Just Humming Along (Pat O'Malley)	28 Apr 1932	Dec F2949	
Lawd, You Made The Night Too Long (Pat O'Malley)	2 May 1932	Dec F2984	
Dream Sweetheart (Pat O'Malley)	17 Jun 1932	Dec F3030	
You're Taking A Chance With Me (Pat O'Malley)	23 Jun 1932	Dec F3040	
After Tonight We Say Goodbye (Pat O'Malley)	4 Oct 1932	Dec F3215	
Can't We Meet Again (And Let's Be Sweethearts?) (Pat O'Malley)	6 Feb 1933	Dec F3459	(88)
You're Mine, You (Pat O'Malley)	30 Jun 1933	Dec F3600	
Did My Heart Beat (Did I Fall In Love?) (Pat O'Mally)	20 Oct 1933	Dec F3715	

The PHILIP LEWIS/RHYTHM MANIACS Sessions, Volume 1 - 1929 : Retrieval FG 410

PHILIP LEWIS AND HIS DANCE ORCHESTRA:		
My Kinda Love (Maurice Elwin)	20 Jun 1929	Dec F1501
My Troubles Are Over (Maurice Elwin)	20 Jun 1929	Dec F1501
A Cute Little Flat (Maurice Elwin)	20 Jun 1929	Dec F1502
Doin' The New Low-Down (Maurice Elwin)	20 Jun 1929	Dec F1502
Jericho (Maurice Elwin)	29 Jun 1929	Dec F1503
There's One Thing Remains (Maurice Elwin)	29 Jun 1929	Dec F1504
Sweetheart Of All My Dreams (Maurice Elwin)	29 Jun 1929	Dec F1503
Down Among The Sugar Cane (take-1) (Maurice Elwin & probably Arthur Lally)	29 Jun 1929	Dec Unissued
Down Among The Sugar Cane (take-2) (Maurice Elwin)	29 Jun 1929	Dec F1504
THE RHYTHM MANIACS:		
Building A Nest For Mary (Maurice Elwin)	16 Jul 1929	Dec F1514
PHILIP LEWIS AND HIS DANCE ORCHESTRA:		
Broadway Melody (Maurice Elwin)	20 Jul 1929	Dec F1508
Diga Diga Doo (Maurice Elwin & probably Arthur Lally)	20 Jul 1929	Dec F1512
What Is This Thing Called Love? (Maurice Elwin)	20 Jul 1929	Dec F1512

THE RHYTHM MANIACS:				
I'm Crooning A Tune About June (Maurice Elwin)	25 Jul 1929	Dec F1515		
That's You, Baby (Maurice Elwin)	25 Jul 1929	Dec F1514		
PHILIP LEWIS AND HIS DANCE ORCHESTRA:				
Imagination Goes A Long Way (Maurice Elwin)	25 Jul 1929	Dec F1513		

Collections

AL BOWLLY - Something To Sing About : EMI Retrospect Series SH 501

GERALDO AND HIS ORCHESTRA:			
Grandma Said (Al Bowlly)	3 Feb 1939	HMV BD5457	
Deep In A Dream (Al Bowlly)	3 Feb 1939	HMV BD5457	(52)
You're A Sweet Little Headache (Al Bowlly)	3 Feb 1939	HMV BD5458	(49)
The Same Old Story (Al Bowlly)	7 Mar 1939	HMV BD5467	(52)
Could Be (Al Bowlly)	7 Mar 1939	HMV BD5468	(52)
Between A Kiss And A Sigh (Al Bowlly)	7 Mar 1939	HMV BD5468	(52)
To Mother With Love (Al Bowlly)	4 Apr 1939	HMV BD5473	
Thanks For Everything (Al Bowlly)	4 Apr 1939	HMV BD5472	(52)
I Miss You In The Morning (Al Bowlly)	4 Apr 1939	HMV BD5473	(52)
MANTOVANI AND HIS ORCHESTRA:			
Something To Sing About (Al Bowlly)	4 Mar 1938	Col FB1925	(109 C84)
In My Little Red Book (Al Bowlly)	4 Mar 1938	Col FB1925	(109 C84)
RONNIE MUNRO AND HIS ORCHESTRA:			
Vieni, Vieni (Al Bowlly)	17 Jul 1937	HMV BD5242	
Le Touquet (Al Bowlly)	17 Jul 1937	HMV BD5242	
Smile When You Say Goodbye (Al Bowlly)	17 Jul 1937	HMV BD5248	
Hometown (Al Bowlly)	17 Jul 1937	HMV BD5248	
REGINALD WILLIAMS AND HIS FUTURISTS:			
I'm Madly In Love With You (Al Bowlly)	8 Feb 1939	Col FB2167	(C33)
Small Town (Al Bowlly)	5 May 1939	Col FB2226	
What Do You Know About Love? (Al Bowlly)	5 May 1939	Col FB2227	

The remaining tracks in this album feature Al Bowlly in a solo capacity (With Orchestra directed by Ronnie Munro). The titles are:-

Moon Love	5 Oct 1939	HMV BD762
Au Revoir, But Not Goodbye	5 Oct 1939	HMV BD762

The Great British Dance Bands Play The Music Of Hugh Charles 1938-1945 - We'll Meet Again : Reid RD 1

ROY FOX AND HIS ORCHESTRA:			
I Won't Tell A Soul (Denny Dennis)	30 Jun 1938	HMV BD5379	
GERALDO AND HIS ORCHESTRA:			
Russian Rose (Dorothy Carless)	26 Aug 1941	Par F1861	
CARROLL GIBBONS AND THE SAVOY HOTEL ORPHEANS:			
The King Is Still In London (Sam Browne)	4 Mar 1941	Col FB2593	
Silver Wings In The Moonlight (Leslie Douglas)	29 Jun 1943	Col FB2945	
JACK HYLTON AND HIS ORCHESTRA:			
Blue Skies Are Round The Corner (Sam Browne)	13 Dec 1938	HMV BD5446	(92)
I Shall Always Remember You Smiling (Peggy Dell)	31 Jan 1939	HMV BD5456	(91)
We'll Meet Again (Dolly Elsie)	29 Nov 1939	HMV BD5540	
KEN "SNAKEHIPS" JOHNSON AND HIS WEST INDIAN ORCHESTRA:			
I'm In Love For The Last Time (Pat O'Regan & Band)	29 Jan 1940	HMV BD5559	

SYDNEY LIPTON AND HIS GROSVENOR HOUSE DANCE ORCHESTRA:				
I Shall Be Waiting (Celia Lipton)	29 Dec 1939	Col FB2359		
Get Into The Spirit Of Spring (Celia Lipton)	24 Apr 1940	Col FB2432		
Memories Live Longer Than Dreams (Eddie Briant)	8 Aug 1940	Col FB2480		
JOE LOSS AND HIS ORCHESTRA:				
There'll Always Be An England (Monte Rey)	2 Nov 1939	RZ MR3173		
A Little King Without A Crown (Paula Green)	31 May 1940	HMV BD5598		
Moonlight And Mimosa (Chick Henderson)	21 Jun 1940	HMV BD5604		
Let The Bands Play (Sam Browne)	12 Dec 1940	HMV BD5640		
When Your Train Has Gone (Paula Green)	4 Feb 1941	HMV BD5657		
FELIX MENDELSSOHN AND HIS HAWAIIAN SERENADERS:				
Where The Waters Are Blue (Alan Kane)	9 Sep 1942	Col FB2855	(115)	
JACK PAYNE WITH HIS ORCHESTRA:				
Till All Our Prayers Are Answered (Jane Lee)	19 Feb 1945	HMV BD5877		
HARRY ROY AND HIS BAND:				
Potato Pete (Harry Roy)	29 May 1941	RZ MR3491		
ERIC WINSTONE AND HIS ACCORDEON BAND:				
There's A Land Of Begin Again (Julie Dawn)	13 Nov 1941	RZ MR3574		

George Gershwin 50th Anniversary Album (1922-1931) : Halcyon HDL 112

BILLY COTTON'S LONDON SAVANNAH BAND:			
'S Wonderful (N/V)	Oct 1928	Pic 142	(C1)
JACK HYLTON AND HIS ORCHESTRA:			
Lady Be Good (Unknown)	29 Mar 1926	HMV B5042	
PERCIVAL MACKEY'S BAND:			
That Certain Feeling (N/V)	19 Aug 1926	Col 4063	
Looking For A Boy (N/V)	19 Aug 1926	Col 4064	(C7 C128)
SAVOY ORPHEANS:			
Fascinating Rhythm (N/V)	23 Mar 1926	HMV B5030	(C7 C128)

The remaining tracks in this album are by the following American bands, playing the titles shown:-

Victor Arden-Phil Ohman & Their Orchestra (Embraceable You)
The Columbians Dance Orchestra (Somebody Loves Me)
The Ipana Troubadours dir. by Sam Lanin (Liza)
Johnny Johnson & His Statler Pennsylvanians (My One And Only)
Roger Wolfe Kahn & His Orchestra (Clap Yo' Hands)
Bert Lown & His Biltimore Hotel Orchestra (Strike Up The Band)
George Olsen & His Music (Do Do Do/Someone To Watch Over Me)
Fred Rich & His Orchestra (I Got Rhythm/The Man I Love)
Ben Selvin & His Orchestra (Oh Gee! Oh Joy!)
Nat Shilkret & His Orchestra (Delishious)
Paul Whiteman & His Orchestra (I'll Build A Stairway To Paradise)

It is understood that the following album is presented free with the Reader's Digest 8-Record Boxed Set "Down Memory Lane - A Salute To The 40's" (See Collection C167). I am indebted to Derek Beeby for the relevant details - E.T.

Golden British Bands Of The 40's : Reader's Digest RDS 10309

AMBROSE AND HIS ORCHESTRA:			
Taking A Chance On Love (Anne Shelton)	21 May 1943	Dec F8313	(16 C104)
BILLY COTTON AND HIS BAND:			
That Lovely Week-End (Dolly Elsie)	3 Dec 1941	Rex 10086	(C105)
GERALDO AND HIS ORCHESTRA:			
The Things We Did Last Summer (Carole Carr)	14 Jan 1947	Par F2205	202

CARROLL GIBBONS AND THE SAVOY HOTEL ORPHEANS:			
I Left My Heart At The Stage Door Canteen (Leslie Douglas)	5 Oct 1943	Col FB2967	(C40)
JACK HYLTON AND HIS ORCHESTRA:			
You've Done Something To My Heart (Bruce Trent)	2 Dec 1939	HMV BD5544	
SYDNEY LIPTON AND HIS GROSVENOR HOUSE DANCE ORCHESTRA:			
Mist On The River (Celia Lipton)	8 Aug 1940	Col FB2480	
JOE LOSS AND HIS ORCHESTRA:			
I Had The Craziest Dream (Harry Kaye)	11 Mar 1943	HMV BD5795	
LOU PREAGER AND HIS ORCHESTA:			
A Garden In The Rain (Paul Rich)	15 Oct 1947	Col FB3355	
OSCAR RABIN AND HIS BAND:			
There Goes That Song Again (Bob Dale)	16 Jun 1941	Rex 10005	(C104)
EDMUNDO ROS AND HIS RUMBA BAND:			
Yours (Quiereme Mucho) (Santiago Lopez)	1 Oct 1941	Par F1892	(C38)
HARRY ROY AND HIS BAND:			
If I Had My Way (Marjorie Kingsley)	23 Oct 1943	RZ MR3717	
THE ROYAL AIR FORCE DANCE ORCHESTRA Directed By Sgt. Jimmy Miller:			
Be Careful, It's My Heart (Jimmy Miller)	11 Sep 1942	Dec F8194	(C105)
THE SKYROCKETS ORCHESTRA Directed By Paul Fenoulhet:			
Imaginez (Doreen Lundy)	9 May 1947	HMV BD5976	
LEW STONE AND HIS BAND:			
Baby Mine (Benny Lee)	20 Jan 1942	Dec F8082	(C104)

ERRATA

The version of "Leicester Square Rag" by Harry Roy and His Orchestra contained in Collection C167 is not the Parlophone recording, as shown against the corresponding Collection number in Section 1 of the Supplement, but the Decca non-vocal version recorded on 27 April 1949 and released on Decca F9145 (164 165).